READ 'EM THEIR WRITES

l c ⁵/₀₉

D0796624

READ 'EM THEIR WRITES

A Handbook for Mystery and Crime Fiction Book Discussions

Gary Warren Niebuhr

LIBRARIES
UNLIMITED
A Member of the Greenwood Publishing Group

Westport, Connecticut • London

Library of Congress Cataloging-in-Publication Data

Niebuhr, Gary Warren.
  Read 'em their writes : a handbook for mystery and crime fiction book discussions / by Gary Warren Niebuhr.
     p. cm.
  Includes bibliographical references and indexes.
  ISBN 1–59158–303–9 (pbk. : alk. paper)
1. Detective and mystery stories—Bibliography.   2. Detective and mystery stories—Stories, plots, etc.   3. Book clubs (Discussion groups)   I. Title.   II. Title: Read them their writes.
Z5917.D5N53   2006
[PN3448.D4]
016.80883'782—dc22   2006012711

British Library Cataloguing in Publication Data is available.

Library of Congress Catalog Card Number: 2006012711
ISBN: 1–59158–303–9

First published in 2006

Libraries Unlimited, 88 Post Road West, Westport, CT 06881
A Member of the Greenwood Publishing Group, Inc.
www.lu.com

Printed in the United States of America

The paper used in this book complies with the Permanent Paper Standard issued by the National Information Standards Organization (Z39.48–1984).

10 9 8 7 6 5 4 3 2 1

For Denice, who has waited patiently for the great American crime novel but is beginning to realize I only intend to read 'em, not write 'em. All my love goes to you for a lifetime of romance and friendship—hubba, hubba!

Contents

Acknowledgments

I consider it a wonder that all my life I have been a reader. My parents and my teachers had an influence on my development, but all of this would have meant nothing if authors had not been producing works that kept challenging my interests and drawing me into their books.

Later in life, I had the opportunity to meet the author of a television novelization that I had read in grade school. The novel's story had appealed to me because the television show had appealed to me. The novel extended that enjoyment onto the printed page. The story I told the author was how I read the book and then passed it on to other boys in my class, each of whom enjoyed the book as much as I did. As I think of it now, it might have been the first book discussion I ever led.

The desire to do a book discussion came from one of the first workshops held by the very new Reader's Advisory Roundtable of the Wisconsin Library Association. The workshop leader: Ted Balcom. Ted's book, *Book Discussion for Adults: A Leader's Guide* (American Library Association, 1992), is still the best overall guide for book discussion leaders. Ted's ability to promote this type of endeavor through his professional approach and his calm demeanor gave me the courage to attempt my first book discussion. This book is a direct result of his wonderful teaching skills.

My library mystery book discussion has the rather unimpressive title of the Greendale Park and Recreation Mystery Book Discussion Group. I have led this mystery book discussion for twelve years. Some of the participants have been with me for the entire run. Each individual who has attended has helped mold the group and given the events their personality, and I want to thank each of them.

On a personal level, I have been able to attend many of the meetings of The Cloak and Clue Society. This mystery book discussion group recently celebrated its twenty-fifth anniversary. This group would never have survived or achieved all that it has without the hard work of Beverly DeWeese. Bev is one of the best book talkers in the library community, and she has taught me many techniques for defining the appeal of a book and broadcasting it to an audience. Her friendship has been invaluable in my development as a professional librarian, a mystery fan, and a book discussion leader.

I would like to thank my two Noirsketeers and partners in crime, Theodore B. Hertel, Jr., and Sandy Balzo, for their continuing guidance and friendship. Their invaluable suggestions in the creation of this work and their hard work in editing it helped define what this book will do.

I would like to thank Barbara Ittner for her patience in nurturing this work through the world of my indifference and procrastination. I would also like to thank Emma Bailey at Libraries Unlimited and Carla L. Talmadge and Deborah Masi at Westchester Book Group for their hard work in producing a useable product out of what I could contribute to the process. Some of the concepts about mysteries may have appeared in my previous work for Libraries Unlimited, *Make Mine a Mystery: A Reader's Guide to Mystery and Detective Fiction* (2003). If you have any suggestions for a revision of this work, please feel free to e-mail me at piesbook@execpc.com.

Introduction

MYSTERY BOOK DISCUSSIONS

Why Mysteries and Crime Fiction Titles Are Discussable

Some people believe that mysteries and crime fiction are not discussable. Here is a quote from the "Book Club How To's" from the Seattle Public Library's Washington Center for the Book:

> During a book discussion, what you're really talking about is everything that the author hasn't said—all those white spaces on the printed page. For this reason, books that are plot driven (most mysteries, westerns, romances, and science fiction/fantasy) don't lend themselves to book discussions. In genre novels and some mainstream fiction, the author spells out everything for the reader, so that there is little to say except, "Gee, I never knew that" or "Isn't that interesting."

I contend that if in the mystery or crime fiction title you have selected "the author spells out everything for the reader," then you have failed to select the right book to discuss.

"[B]ooks that are plot driven . . . don't lend themselves to book discussions" is a true statement in any genre. However, this does not exclude all mysteries or crime fiction as sources for a great book discussion. Some mysteries have a theme equal to any contained in contemporary fiction, and in combination with a challenging and thrilling plot, wonderfully developed characters, and interesting settings, will make fine book discussion titles.

Many classic mystery fiction titles (those written in the Golden Age style) are not good selections for mystery book discussions. The basic concept of most traditional Golden Age novels is that the reader is willing to play a game against the author. The author's job is to create a mystery puzzle with confusing details that the fictional detective will try to unravel. The author must "play fair," or allow the reader to see the detective discover the clues needed to solve the crime, but the author is allowed to lace the book with "red herrings," or false clues, to deceive the reader. A well-written mystery novel from the Golden Age is defined as one that allows the author's fictional detective to reveal the solution to the crime before the reader discovers the correct solution. This revelation usually takes place in some culminating scene in the novel, leading to the creation of the "gathering of the suspects" chapter.

This classic pattern is great fun for recreational reading, but does not offer much for a contemporary book discussion. It is too plot driven, and the characters are rarely developed to a point of being discussable. Contemporary writers continue to write novels in this style. Although these books are fine entertainment, they do not work for our purposes—with one exception. That would be in the case of the fan mystery book discussion group that is reading these titles because of its acceptance of the restrictions of the genre.

When you hear the maxim that in a book discussion, "what you're really talking about is everything that the author hasn't said," you should carefully examine the mystery or crime fiction title being considered to see if it engages the reader in more areas than just the plot.

Can the way a book is written affect the reader? Does its action, its tone, its very construction create different appeals for readers? In the mystery and crime fiction field, the answer is a resounding yes. Levels of action make various requirements of mystery readers, and the effect can be positive or negative for a book discussion depending on how it creates "all those white spaces." Here are three levels of action present in mystery and crime fiction titles.

> In a **soft-boiled (or cozy) novel**, the action is low on the description of violence, with little overt sexual content or abusive language. A soft-boiled world is one in which society is viewed as orderly and controlled, and the crime is a failure of the society to function correctly. The society portrayed is often a closed or confined set. The inclusion of a mystery in a soft-boiled world is an intrusion. Most violent action takes place off-stage. The emphasis is on the solution of the crime. Readers anticipate a world where right and wrong are clearly defined. The society depicted in a soft-boiled novel is more moral than in a hard-boiled world, and the reader expects the detective to follow clues left by the perpetrator to an eventual administration of justice. The detective is often an amateur, although protagonists are not limited to this type of detective. The risk in using a soft-boiled novel is that the plot dominates and the supporting characteristics (character development, setting, theme, etc.) are generally not strong enough to promote a good discussion. While these novels are great entertainment, I suggest that most soft-boiled mystery and crime fiction novels do not make good book discussion titles. The exception is for groups whose

focus is to read mystery or crime fiction as fans to honor the history of this genre or to better understand or enjoy the contemporary writers working in this field. This observation should not be taken as a directive never to use soft-boiled novels, and, in fact, among the titles suggested in the upcoming chapter, some soft-boiled novels are listed for groups who are not comfortable with some of the elements contained in a traditional or hard-boiled novel.

In a **traditional novel**, the author employs action and violence to establish the seriousness of the crime without trivializing its importance or glorifying its horrifying effects. Although most violent action takes place on-stage, it is not graphically described. The emphasis can be equally on the perpetration and solution of the crime. The protagonist's goal is to find a solution to the crime, but not necessarily through the administration of justice by an official court of law. Nonetheless, the intent of a traditional novel is to restore the balance of right and wrong in a society gone wrong. The ambiguities that begin to appear in this style of mystery or crime fiction, in contrast to the more rigidly defined world of the soft-boiled, mean the titles are generally more suited for book discussions.

In a **hard-boiled novel**, the action is high on the description of violence, as well as sexual content and the language of the streets. In a hard-boiled world, everyone and everything is suspect, including established institutions and the people who work for them, even the legal forces. The inclusion of a mystery in a hard-boiled world is inevitable. Most violent action takes place on-stage. The emphasis is on the perpetration of the crime, and characters are often driven to do what they do by circumstances that are often out of their control. Hard-boiled novels sometimes feature protagonists who are not clearly defined as being on either the right or wrong side of the law. The administration of justice is not certain in a hard-boiled novel, and morality may have many definitions in a hard-boiled world. I contend that the novels in the hard-boiled style of mystery and crime fiction make the best book discussion titles because they contain the highest level of "all those white spaces on the printed page."

Before beginning a book discussion in this genre, you should realize that mystery and crime fiction deals with death and a society out of control. To examine this literature, participants must be willing to look at dark, ugly subjects that may extend the boundaries they have set regarding the use of language, sex, and violence. While a less-controversial book might make a "good" read, it will not challenge the participants to express their opinions like a fiercely written traditional or hard-boiled novel.

Many books in the mystery and crime fiction genre feature characters that continue to appear in a series of novels. If you plan to consider a series novel, make sure the title you select has a series character who grows as a person within the context of the book selected. Static characters in a series context are not interesting enough to discuss.

A mystery and crime fiction book discussion can be organized in a number of ways. Like all book discussions, a title can be selected for a one-time, drop-in book discussion. A more challenging structure involves a group discussing all the titles in one series of an author, all the books of one author who does not write series titles, a particular style of mystery or crime fiction novel, or mystery and crime fiction titles that share a common theme. Of course, good old random choice would work as well.

The Subgenres of Mystery and Crime Fiction

Before establishing a book discussion on a title from the mystery and crime fiction genre, you should have a basic understanding of the types of subgenres that exist within this style of literature.

What is a *mystery*?
A mystery is a work of fiction in which the reader is asked to help solve a puzzle. The essential ingredients are an element of crime mixed with an element of detection.

What is a *detective novel*?
A detective novel is a mystery in which a fictional character tries to solve the puzzle before the reader does. It is an intellectual exercise. The concept is that the author will "play fair" with the reader by providing clues. It is fair for the author to use "red herrings" to distract the reader. The central question is "whodunit?"

What is a *crime novel*?
A crime novel observes the undertaking of a criminal act, but does not necessarily have a detective who pursues either the criminal or a sense of justice.

What is *intrigue*?
In a novel of intrigue, the goal is accomplished by devious means.

What is *suspense*?
A work of suspense keeps the reader waiting for particular outcomes, often by having the narrator in some kind of danger, even if it is a detective. It is also an emotional experience. Suspense poses a threat to a character who is often the primary victim of the evil. The central question is "whom is it going to happen to?"

What is *adventure*?
Dangerous actions or risks are undertaken in an adventure novel.

What is a *thriller*?

A thriller is fiction designed to keep the reader interested through the use of a high degree of action, intrigue, adventure, and suspense. A thriller involves the reader emotionally.

Selecting the Mystery and Crime Fiction Titles to Discuss

What should you look for in a mystery or crime novel when considering it for selection?

A good place to start is with titles that have received critical recognition. The mystery fan community recognizes excellence by a variety of methods ranging from lists of "best" books to annual awards. Remember that just because a book is an award winner does not mean it will be discussable. The criteria listed below the award sites should still be applied in the decision-making process.

Complete access to award information for crime and mystery fiction titles can be found at

- http://www.cluelass.com

The individual awards are listed at:

- Agatha Awards: http://users.erols.com/malice
- Anthony Awards: http://www.bouchercon.info
- Barry Awards: http://www.deadlypleasures.com/Barry.htm
- Dagger Awards: http://www.kjm.org/cwa.htm
- Dilys Award: http://www.mysterybooksellers.com/dilys.html
- Edgar Awards: http://www.mysterywriters.org/awards.html
- Ellis Awards: http://www.crimewriterscanada.com
- Hammett Awards: http://www.hycyber.com/MYST/hammetts.html
- Macavity Awards: http://www.mysteryreaders.org/macavity.html
- Kelly Awards: http://www.thecwaa.net
- Shamus Awards: http://www.thrillingdetective.com/trivia/triv72.html

The best way to find suggested titles is by reading reviews. While professional reviews have validity, the mystery and crime fiction fan community does a great job of tracking and reviewing titles in the genre. Please access the fan review sources listed at the end of the book.

Here are some questions to ask when determining if a book would work as a discussion title. Some of the characteristics mentioned can be determined from reading reviews, but the best test case will be to read all or part of the text.

- Author—Is the author well respected in the field? Has the author won awards? Is he/she a bestselling author? If this is the author's first novel, did it get a great review?
- Plot—Is the crime compelling by its nature? Is the plot believable? Are there enough clues? Does the plot play fair? Does the plot hold your interest? Do you care whodunit? Do you care whydunnit?
- Subplots—Are there threads to the plot that were as compelling to read as the mystery/crime?
- Main Character—Do you care what happened to this character? Do you understand what happened to this character? Do you agree with what happened to this character? Do you identify with this character? Is this character heroic? Are the character's decisions and actions believably motivated? Is there something about this character that you cannot understand?
- Secondary Characters—Do you care what happened to these characters? Do you understand what happened to all of the characters? Do you agree with what happened to all of the characters? Do you identify with one of the secondary characters? Are any of the secondary characters heroic? Are the secondary characters' decisions and actions believably motivated? Is there something about any of the secondary characters that you cannot understand?
- Subject—Is this book about some life experience outside of the mystery/crime? Does this novel teach you anything new?
- Setting—Is the setting of this novel interesting? Are there elements within the setting that taught you something new?
- Time Period—Does this novel hold a mirror up to a particular time period? Are there elements in the time period that taught you something new?
- Structure—Is there something unique or challenging in the structure of this novel?
- Style—Is there something unique or challenging in the style of this novel?
- Theme—Does this novel make you consider an element of life from a new angle? Does this novel challenge your opinion or perspective on an element of life? Does this novel raise your emotional level?

AN OVERVIEW OF THIS BOOK

Read 'Em Their Writes: A Handbook for Mystery and Crime Fiction Book Discussions is a guide for those who wish to begin or maintain a mystery book club—in a library, in a bookstore, or in the comfort of their own home. You'll learn how to conduct a quality book discussion using titles from the mystery and crime genre. Basic instructions for running any book discussion are included, ranging from selecting the leader, to finding the participants, choosing the title, and conducting the discussion. However, remember that while basic concepts are good, every book discussion group takes on the personality of those who participate. Flexibility in regard to these concepts will lead to a satisfying experience for all participants. This work shows you how to use your own creativity to produce a rich experience for those who participate in your discussion.

In 2004, there were 25,184 adult fiction titles published according to the survey produced by Bowker. According to the statistics maintained by the Romance Writers of America, popular fiction sales figures for 2004 are as follows:

- Romance fiction, 33.8 percent
- Mystery/detective/suspense fiction, 25.6 percent
- General fiction, 24.9 percent
- Science fiction, 6 percent
- All other types, 9.7 percent

These statistics make the popularity of the mystery genre clear, and should give you the encouragement to become a mystery book discussion leader. This book can help you develop the basic skills you need. If you do not want to lead the discussion, you'll find some suggestions for selecting a leader or avoiding having a leader altogether. Once you have decided on the goals of the group, this guide can help you find other readers with similar interests who want to meet and discuss the titles you have selected for the discussion.

This guide also helps you select titles that work well for discussion. A wide range of titles are suggested here, from traditional mysteries through crime novels all the way to works of literature with a hint of crime. What works for a mystery and crime book discussion may or may not fit most people's definition of titles in this genre. I argue that a genre-specific label for the group should not stop a good book discussion leader from sneaking in surprising titles that expand the reading interests of the participants. You'll also learn why some types of mysteries will never be good book discussion titles.

For each book suggested, you will find a model for conducting the discussion that includes the following:

- Author
- Title
- Publication date
- Number of pages
- Geographic setting
- Time period

- Series notes
- Plot summary
- Subject headings
- Appeal points
- Similar works
- Discussion questions

One hundred solid book discussion titles are offered, along with background information on the author and book, as well as specific discussion questions. These are titles that I have read and field-tested in my own mystery book discussions. Following that, an additional fifty potential book discussion titles are listed. These books have received reviews or awards that would recommend them for use in a book discussion. After you become an experienced book discussion leader, or if you have the skills now, you will be able to create your own pathways through these novels. The Resources for Crime and Mystery Book Discussion Leaders section provides sources for determining your own books likely to make great mystery and crime book discussion titles.

Even if you are an experienced book discussion leader, certain aspects of this genre that are unique to it require a special style when leading a discussion. Although I am a librarian and therefore my focus will be on library mystery and crime fiction book discussions, this guide can easily be used by any book discussion leader interested in starting a mystery and crime fiction book discussion. There is no environment inappropriate for holding a book discussion whether it is a private home, a nursing home, a church, a social organization, or a school.

WHY TALK ABOUT BOOKS?

Reading, by its nature, is a solitary activity. However, reading a book opens a person to new possibilities:

- Have you ever read a passage in a book that is so good that you had to read it out loud to someone else?
- Have you ever felt the need to discuss something you read in a book with a friend or two?
- Do you have questions after reading a book that you need to ask your friends?
- Have you ever disliked a book so much that you had to let someone else know why?

What human activity can be more American than the desire to gather for social discourse? We may be isolated in individual activities, yet as humans we are always trying to gather back into social units. While surfing the Internet, we participate in listservs or Web logs (blogs) in order to bond with our fellow humans. We even talk out loud in a movie or theater production, unable to sit still and enjoy a performance without trying to share our response with the people around us. We now use our cell phones to instantaneously share an experience with someone else wherever we are. This is the desire that a good book discussion leader taps into when creating the environment needed to discuss an exciting book.

Why talk about mystery and crime fiction? Every book you select for a book discussion should be

- Interesting to read
- Mystifying in its presentation
- Challenging in its theme

Mystery and crime fiction is interesting to read because it involves the disruption of society and, almost always, a death. Authors in this genre are masters at creating a story within the context of normality and twisting events into an intriguing work of literature. There is an inherent tension in this kind of story because it is about issues that most of us would hope to avoid in our lives. Character is essential to all mystery and crime fiction titles, whether we are following the exploits of a master detective, chilled by the horrifying acts of a murderer or fascinated by the behavior of those who commit crimes.

A traditional whodunit is intriguing only because of its construction. It may make great leisure reading, but a clue-driven puzzle novel is not necessarily a great title to select for discussion. The exception would be mystery book discussions looking at a clue-driven puzzle because of an interest in that specific genre.

Mystification in a traditional mystery should not be limited to plot, but must also have strength in these areas:

- Character
- Setting
- Pace
- Theme

In contrast to the traditional mystery is the crime fiction novel in which the plot is equal or subordinate to the question of whydunnit. Whydunnits usually make the best mystery and crime fiction book discussion titles. Commission of a crime is antisocial behavior and within itself is compelling to discuss as a feature of the plot. Combine that with great characters who mystify us as to why they have acted in this fashion and a theme that challenges the reader to think about life, not just the crime.

With all these elements in place and all the answers elusive, you have a solid selection to discuss. The best mystery and crime fiction titles to discuss are those where

- the detective tells us all about the solving of the case but remains mystified as to the cause until the very end,
- the people who are featured have some mystifying aspects to their characters,
- the author has something to tell us about the meaning of life other than people should not kill each other,
- the emotional response to reading the book gave you the need to talk to someone about it.

GENERAL BOOK DISCUSSION PROCEDURES

Leading a Book Discussion

Who will lead your discussion group and how are important issues to consider. Leadership styles are as diverse as the titles that will be read. Here are a few of the leadership styles that can be adopted for a book discussion.

The **benign dictatorship** solves most problems, at least for the fearless leader. If you decide to lead the group by making all the decisions, be prepared to do all the work. Besides having the responsibility to create the needed components, your attendance becomes an issue. Without you, the group fails.

Once the membership of the group is established, **rotating the responsibility** is a fairly common practice for the leadership. Each session, a different member assumes the mantle of leader. The benefit is that the burden of the work is shared. The caution is that the group is now dependent on a number of individuals with a variety of skills, desire, and dependability.

Some groups prefer **no leader**. This style can range from anarchy (i.e., let's drink wine and never actually discuss the book) to democracy (each member of the group brings one question to ask the group). Ultimately, even when a decision is made to have no leader, there must be some process to deal with all the other incumbent needs of a book discussion group (see the following sections) in order to make it a success.

Bringing in an outside book discussion leader is a possibility for groups that are created by an institution unwilling to foster or provide a leader from its own. The **hired gun** can bring a fresh perspective to the discussion. The caution is that hired guns are often mistaken for lecturers rather than discussion leaders and the participants may not be as willing to challenge a stranger as they might a familiar face.

Selecting the Book to Be Discussed

As the benign dictator, you can just pick a book. Love me or leave me. Problem solved.

When an individual member's number comes up in a group that rotates the responsibility, he/she can choose the title. When an outside discussion leader is used, those hiring him/her can select the title, or the hired gun may make suggestions.

In a group that has no leader, a title will have to be selected by whatever democratic practice the group wants to invent. Each member can suggest titles that go into a pool from which new books to discuss are picked. A survey can be created and the group can hold an election for the titles to be read.

No matter who is making the decision, there are some things your group needs to decide before selecting the title. One basic decision that must be made is what type of reading the group will be doing. Some groups love the anarchy of never knowing what kind of book will be read next. Others may want to define the reading interests. An example is limiting reading selections to fiction titles to the exclusion of nonfiction.

The theme for this book is mystery and crime fiction, but whether the chosen theme for a book discussion is Great Books, Women's Fiction, or Oprah's Titles, that theme defines what type of books will be read at each session.

Before your group selects a title, the book discussion leader should research the availability of the title. The book either has to be in print, available at used bookstores, or on the shelves of the local library. Some groups are organized so they can provide the title to the participants through library operations like interlibrary loan, or by purchasing the titles in advance either from the participants' registration fees or through a book discussion grant.

The timing of book selection is also important. Is a meeting schedule set for the year, with the titles listed? Does the group decide month by month what titles will be read? Remember that not all members of the group can read at the same speed. Some members will want to start reading much earlier than others, especially if they want to read the title twice in order to understand it better. (This can also be true of the discussion leader.)

Whatever books you pick, try to ensure that they have interesting plots, well-developed characters, unusual settings, and strong themes. Do not be afraid to read outside your own personal interests. One of the most enriching things about a book discussion is to read a title you would not have selected yourself.

Deciding Who, Where, When, and How to Meet

Who

Before initiating a book discussion group, you need to think about who will be allowed to participate and how they will be recruited. Once the group is established, you must think about how the group will be maintained and grown.

The group should decide:

- Who is going to be allowed to attend the discussion?
- Is this an adults-only group, senior specific, or open to anyone who drops in?

- Will there be advance registration or will it be free to anyone who drops in?
- How many people are you going to allow to join the discussion group?
- How will the group stay in touch—by telephone, e-mail, Web site?

A solid rule of thumb is that ten to fifteen people make an ideal group size.

Where

The purpose of the book discussion group may dictate the best place to meet. One of the mystery and crime book discussions I attend meets in a church each month. It does, at times, seem an odd contrast between our environment and some of the issues we discuss, but it serves our needs well.

What is important? The location should be convenient and safe for the attendees in the sense that it provides an environment for casual group conversation without barriers. Privacy for the group is important so that opinions can be expressed.

When

I have participated in one-time discussions, monthly events, and weekly meetings. Each has worked for its own reasons. Your group needs to establish a meeting pattern that does not overburden the members, but gives them time to read the titles selected, and encourages them to attend regularly.

How

Classroom settings should be avoided to prevent the discussion from taking on the feeling of an assignment. If a classroom is used, the classroom setup of the chairs is a thing to avoid. Chairs arranged in a circle is best, even if it is around a table. It is essential for all members to hear each other.

The day of the week, the time of the day, and the length of the meeting can either encourage or discourage participation. Is food going to be served? Are beverages, even alcohol, going to be allowed? Remember to build in some social time for the group so that the members can truly build connections, especially if this is an ongoing series.

Do not overlook the fact that you might have some expenses in operating a book discussion group. Establishing a budget and a membership fee may be necessary to ensure longevity for the group.

GENERAL BOOK DISCUSSION LEADER PROCEDURES

Preparing for the Discussion

As leader, you need to accept the responsibility to prepare in advance of the discussion. The more preparation you do, the better the discussion will go. Each time you prepare, the process will become more routine and less of a burden. Just as the goal is to provide an enjoyable experience for those who attend, you should have fun as well. Avoid the danger of overpreparing or making the leadership role seem like a class assignment.

With that said, **you must read the book** at least once. Some book discussion manuals will tell you to read it twice! I would suggest that your job is to lead a discussion on the book, not memorize it.

Take notes while reading. The notes could include:

- A list of characters
- A one sentence synopsis of the plot developments in each chapter
- Unfamiliar terms, languages, locations, or historical references in the text
- Quotes from the text
- Questions to ask the group

Look up anything unfamiliar in the text. If you have a question about something in the text, so will someone else in the group. It helps if all of your references include the page number on which they occur so they can be easily found in the text during the discussion.

Do some homework. Learn something about the author. Examples of information to be shared include biographical information, a bibliography of the author's works, awards the author has received and the author's Web site information.

Learn something about the book. Even the publisher may tell you something about it. In addition, some publishers' Web sites now contain reader's guides that include book discussion questions.

Reading reviews about the title will help you with your preparation and may give you hints as to what questions to ask. Generally, avoid quoting from a review until the end of the discussion, in order to prevent prejudicing the opinions of the participants. However, if the comments made in a review become relevant to a particular aspect of the book being discussed, by all means, reference the review.

Learn something about the genre or subgenre that your book fits into. The purpose of this guide is to help you discuss books in the mystery and crime fiction field, so looking at resources and Web sites about this genre will help you better understand the context of the work and enhance your ability to lead a discussion. Make sure you check the Web sites and other resources listed in the Resources for Mystery and Crime Book Discussion Leaders section of this book.

After doing all this research, you will be tempted to turn the discussion into a lecture so you can reveal all you learned about the author or the book. Never miss an opportunity to ask a good question or to elicit a question from the group. If you are excited about something, lead the group to that point with a question. During the discussion, make sure you do not prejudice the participants with your research or the conclusions reached by reviews. The purpose of the research is to make you a book discussion facilitator, not to mold or lead the participants to a particular conclusion.

In a book discussion, one of the goals is to make everyone feel there are no wrong answers. The only exception is factual issues that can be documented in the text.

Preparing to Ask the Questions

As you read the book, questions will arise. Write these down as they occur and note the page, or even the paragraph on the page, that generated the question. This will help you during the discussion to refer back to the text for support or clarification. Be an overachiever, and think of as many questions as you can. You don't have to use them all, but it's great to have choices to use as the discussion meanders over different topics. A good rule of thumb is to have one question for every five minutes that the group is going to meet.

Your questions should be open-ended, structured so that the answer is not just a "yes" or "no." If you have a yes/no question that you just have to ask, make sure you add the word "why" to the questions.

> AVOID: Can Gary be blamed for the consequences of his actions?
> Answer: Yes.
> Answer: No.

> BETTER: Why can Gary be blamed for the consequences of his actions?
> Answer: Because...

Follow-up questions are vital. In the above scenario, when the "better" question is asked, does it not assume that Gary can be blamed? So, have a follow-up question:

> FOLLOW-UP: Is it fair that Gary is blamed for the consequences of his actions?

This allows those too timid to disagree with the original question or their fellow participants to have an open door inviting them to walk through.

If one strong opinion is expressed during a discussion, a great follow-up question is:

> FOLLOW-UP: Does everyone else agree with that?

Keeping everyone involved by granting them permission to speak is a very positive role of the leader.

In creating questions, do not shy away from the controversial in the text. These issues may create the best questions of the discussion and might be the very issues that your participants have come to discuss. Although factual questions are good, try to develop questions dealing with the book's major themes. Design your questions so they have less of an academic tone and are not constructed to confuse. The questions should make the group think and respond. Try to avoid creating questions that lead the group to an answer within the question itself (unless that is your hidden plan).

> ACADEMIC: Does Gary's inability to accept the consequences of his own actions echo Shakespeare's theme in *Macbeth*?

> BETTER: Does Gary's inability to accept the consequences of his own actions remind you of any books you have read?

Try to structure the questions so that they build in tempo. The participants may want to discuss the major theme of the book at the very beginning, but like a great jockey, you must lead your racehorse to the finish line.

Sooner or later, you are going to be caught short or without any questions at all. One technique for developing questions is to have a piece of paper and a pencil handy for each participant. Ask them to write down a question that they would like to discuss. I have used this technique when called in at the last minute to substitute for a discussion leader when I did not read the book!

Another method you might try is word association. Have each participant write down one word (or one sentence) that describes the book. You can generate a discussion by reading these single words to the group.

It is possible that a trained book discussion leader could lead each time without reading the title. There is a standard list of questions that can be asked that will keep the discussion going. Please note that these questions are designed to build momentum in the book discussion.

- Standard questions:
    Were the characters believable?

    To which character could you most relate?

    Was the plot believable?

    What scene from this book do you like most—or least?

    Did the book's setting enhance the story?

    What do you think happened to these characters after the book ended?

    How did you feel at the end of the book?

    Was order restored to this world at the end of the novel?

    Was justice obtained at the end of the novel?

    Did you enjoy the author's style?

    What do you think the title meant?

What was the book's theme?

Did the theme affect any of the main characters?

Can you name another book that this book compares to?

- Standard follow-up questions for all responses by participants:

Why?

Does everyone agree with that?

- Standard follow-up when a participant raises his/her own question to you:

What do you think?

- Standard filler questions:

Who would you cast in the movie version of this book?

Would you read another book by this author?

Theoretically, if you walked cold into a room and asked these questions of the participants, a one-hour book discussion would ensue.

However, I do not advocate this method, except in emergencies. Every book discussion leader should take some time to think about the process and to become personally involved in each discussion, even if it is just determining the value of questions borrowed from another source. This makes for a dynamic discussion, and it is also more fun for the leader.

This guide provides questions for those book discussion leaders who are short on time to develop their own set of questions. Some libraries and other sources also list their questions on the Web. There is no shame in borrowing from another source for good book discussion questions, but give your list some thought. And make sure you use the resources listed at the end of this book to help develop your questions.

Running the Discussion

Each discussion group functions differently, depending partly on the type of discussion selected by the group. For one-time or drop-in events, it is a great idea to begin by having each person briefly introduce him/herself. You might suggest what they should say, such as why they are there or what they like to read. This gets your participants used to talking, which should help when the discussion begins. Remember, you do not want to waste too much time here. Make it brief, keep it lively, and get on with the book discussion.

You can open with an overview of the type of book selected and the genre it belongs to. Give a brief overview of the author. I like to prepare a handout that contains some background information on the author and the book. (For a sample of one of these handouts, please see the Appendix.) If you do prepare a handout in advance, create some informal notes for yourself. Most of the details can be contained on that, and you only need to hit the high points. Remember, you are not there to give a lecture.

Use the questions you have prepared in advance as needed. While the basic idea is that you have one open-ended question for every five minutes of the discussion, the questions are for your guidance. They are not a strict outline. If the participants get on a roll, let them go as long as they stay on the topic of the book. There is no problem with participants thinking up their own questions. If questions from the group are coming too fast to allow a proper discussion on each one, let the participants know that you are writing down the questions to remember them and that you will get back to them when the discussion slackens. The best book discussion is the one where you are reduced to the role of a tennis chair umpire.

Even if you have organized your questions in a logical progression, don't get upset if you lose track, as long as the discussion is moving forward. And don't get upset if one of the participants anticipates a great question you have developed, or thinks of a question you did not. Instead, when the participants ask their own questions, write them down. Good book discussion leaders know these new questions can be used the next time they lead a discussion on this title.

Participants may directly confront you because of a particular question, putting you in the position of being the ultimate authority. Remember what a psychiatrist does when directly challenged? He/she asks, "What do you think?" To deflect the challenge away from you, ask, "What does the group think?"

On the other hand, part of your role is disciplinarian. Do not let one person dominate the group. Pay attention to body language and eye contact amongst the participants. Try to avoid questions of right and wrong unless they are dealing with factual information from the book. Try to keep the comments relevant to the text and avoid wandering off into discussions on topics not relevant to the text.

GENERAL BOOK DISCUSSION PARTICIPANT PROCEDURES

As a book discussion leader, it is fair for you to have an expectation level for the participants. It is also fair for you to share these expectations with the group at the beginning of the book discussion. They include:

- Obtaining and reading the book prior to the discussion
- Coming to the discussion willing to share opinions
- Coming to the discussion willing to listen to the opinions of the other participants

Encourage participants to attend even if they did not like the book. Remind them that a group split in their opinions makes for a more interesting discussion. Advise participants, if they do not like the current selection, to read at least the first 100 pages and come ready to share with others what kept them from being able to finish the book. Sometimes, after the discussion, participants may find that they want to go back and finish the book.

It is never required that each individual speak. Of course, the hope is that each person will be willing to enhance the experience by sharing a point of view. Participants' comments should be relevant to the book and not sidetrack the discussion. All opinions about the text are valid, and each participant should respect fellow attendees. Remind the group that there is no truth when discussing a book. There are no right answers.

Participants should not hold private conversations away from the main discussion. All comments about the text should be shared with the group.

All participants read the same words, but each reads a different book. Make sure you do your best to give everyone a chance to share what they have read.

100 Mystery and Crime Fiction
Books to Discuss

Margery Allingham

The Tiger in the Smoke

Margery Allingham was born in Ealing, England, to parents who were writers. Her first publication was a story called "Blackkerchief Dick," published in 1923 when she was just nineteen years old. Her first mystery novel, *The White Cottage Mystery,* was published in 1928. In 1929, Allingham's famous series detective, Albert Campion, first appeared as a minor character in *The Crime at Black Dudley* (U.S. title: *The Black Dudley Murder*). Eventually, twenty-five novels were published in the Campion series. *The Tiger in the Smoke*, considered by some to be her greatest work, finds Campion a minor character as well. Her final novel, *Cargo of Eagles*, was published after her death in 1965, as were two Campion novels written by Philip Youngman Carter, her husband since 1927.

Plot summary: Meg Elginbrodde's husband, Major Martin Elginbrodde, was killed during World War II, and she is now preparing to move on with her life by marrying Geoffrey Levett. But five years after Elginbrodde's supposed death, someone begins to send her pictures of him wandering the streets of London. Calling in the amateur detective Albert Campion also gets D.C.I. Charles Luke involved in the case, and an investigation is launched that will expose the damages inflicted on the people of England in their long conflict during World War II.

> **Web site:**
> http://www.margeryallingham
> .org.uk
> **Reader's guide:**
> none

Publication date: 1952

Number of pages: 254

Geographic setting: England, London

Time period: 1950s

Series notes: This is book sixteen in a series of twenty-five. Albert Campion is an eccentric amateur with a royal background and possible covert duty in His Majesty's Service. In the early titles, his odd behavior is used to his advantage as a detective, placing him outside the normal sphere, and thus able to carry out investigations without interference. In later titles he matures into a more humane character, and he allies himself with Scotland Yard Inspectors Oates, Yeo, and Luke. The series also features a love story between Campion and Lady Amanda Fitton. In some of the later books Campion does not appear until near the end of the novel. This novel works well for groups looking for a cozy style or gentle read mystery.

> **Readalikes**
>
> Evelyn Anthony—similar use of suspense
>
> Alistair MacLean—similar use of a wartime theme
>
> Ngaio Marsh—similar style of detective

Subject headings: War—psychological effects; Widows

Appeal points: This book appeals to readers who enjoy the traditional mystery novel. While earlier books in this series fit the Golden Age style, this novel shows how Allingham adapted to the inclusion of psychological tension that became a part of mystery fiction in the 1950s. The book has little dependence on the series character, so series familiarity is not necessary.

DISCUSSION QUESTIONS

How large a role does Albert Campion play in this novel?

What role does fog play in this novel?

What sense of the effect of World War II appears in this story?

Is the Canon crazy like a fox?

Why does the Canon sacrifice himself to the Gaffer?

What is the Science of Life?

Are we predestined to be evil or do we make a choice?

Is the treasure worth the effort to retrieve it?

Is justice served at the end of the novel?

What creates a boy like Johnny Cash, and how can we prevent boys like him?

See standard questions in the Introduction for more questions.

◇◇◆◇◇

Eric Ambler

A Coffin for Dimitrios (British title: The Mask of Dimitrios)

Born in 1909 in London, England, Eric Ambler was the son of music-hall performers. He attended the Northampton Polytechnic branch of University of London from 1924 to 1927, but left before graduating. Ambler worked in various careers—as an engineering apprentice, a vaudevillian, and an advertising man. From 1940 until 1946 he served in the British Army's artillery corps. His first novel, *The Dark Frontier*, appeared in 1936. Over the course of his career, he received an Academy Award nomination for the screenplay *The Cruel Sea*, a Golden Dagger for *A Passage of Arms*, *The Light of Day* (also an Edgar Award), *Dirty Story*, and *The Levanter*. The Mystery Writers of America made Ambler a Grand Master in 1975, and the Crime Writers' Association gave him the Diamond Dagger for lifetime achievement in 1986. He was married twice. Ambler died in 1998.

> **Web site:**
> none
> **Reader's guide:**
> none

Plot summary: Charles Latimer, an author of mysteries, is traveling when he meets Turkish Colonel Haki, a fan of Latimer's espionage novels. Haki shares a tale of master criminal Dimitrios Makropolous, whose story so fascinates Latimer that he begins to search for the truth about this criminal. As the search progresses, Latimer begins to wonder if he is the victim of a masterful manipulation.

Publication date: 1939

Number of pages: 304

Geographic setting: Balkans; Turkey, Istanbul

Time period: 1930s

Series notes: This is a stand-alone novel.

Subject headings: Authors; Espionage

Appeal points: This early example of espionage writing still has a sense of suspense that entertains and engages readers. The constant question of who is manipulating whom usually keeps the attention of all readers.

> **Readalikes**
>
> Erskine Childers' *The Riddle of the Sands*—similar use of espionage
>
> Alan Furst—similar incorporation of espionage and war
>
> Graham Greene's *The Third Man*—similar sense of paranoia

DISCUSSION QUESTIONS

What is Colonel Haki's real goal?

"I wonder if you are interested in real murderers, Mr. Latimer," asks Colonel Haki. How close to his subject should an author get?

What elements of the Latimer character make him a perfect foil for the journey of discovery?

Who is betrayed in this novel?

Does money make the man, or are criminals like Dimitrios destined from birth?

What part of the 1922 pogrom he escapes from helps make Dimitrios the man he becomes?

How much of Dimitrios is just a part of the "system"?

What should society do with a man like Dimitrios?

See standard questions in the Introduction for more questions.

◇◇◆◇◇

Margaret Atwood

The Blind Assassin

Margaret Atwood was born on November 18, 1939, in Ottawa, Canada. She has a B.A. from the University of Toronto and an M.A. from Radcliffe College in Cambridge, Massachusetts. From 1964 until 1989, Atwood taught in various university settings. She holds sixteen honorary degrees from various universities around the world. Living in Toronto, Canada, she is a full-time writer.

Plot summary: "Ten days after the war ended, my sister drove a car off the bridge." After that compelling opening sentence, Iris, an elderly woman suffering a heart condition, begins to tell the story of her sister Laura. Laura's death in 1945, ruled an accident, is only the beginning of a family history that includes death, false love, and greed. Mysterious elements are introduced in Iris' life including the strange disappearance of her husband in a sailing accident and the death of Iris' daughter. The novel also introduces a science fiction work called *The Blind Assassin*—a book within the book. A companion story to Iris' reminiscences, this story eventually proves to be as much about Iris' life as it is a lavish tale of science fiction pulp writing. Atwood's complex novel intrigues readers, and finally reveals the horrific truths behind the incidents in Iris' life.

> **Web site:**
> http://www.owtoad.com
> **Reader's guide:**
> http://www.randomhouse.
> com/catalog/display.pperl?isbn=
> 9780385475723&view=rg

Publication date: 2000

Number of pages: 521

Geographic setting: Canada, Port Ticonderoga

Time period: 1920s, 1930s, 1940s

Series notes: This is a stand-alone novel.

Subject headings: Depression (1929–1939); Sisters; Widows

Appeal points: This is a great work of literature that has virtually nothing to do with mystery fiction as it is normally defined. Yet, the deaths and their mysterious surroundings do hold the interest of many mystery readers. This novel is an example of how a book discussion leader can extend the definition of "mystery" and sneak in a work of contemporary fiction. It also has the element of science fiction. Remember, not all mystery and crime fiction novels have to be about murder. This novel was awarded the Booker Prize and the Dashiell Hammett Award by the International Association of Crime Writers.

> **Readalikes**
>
> Louis de Bernieres' *Corelli's Mandolin*—similar effect of major theme on character development
>
> Anita Shreve—similar stylist
>
> Anne Tyler—similar complex themes based on family structures

DISCUSSION QUESTIONS

This novel is all about hidden meanings in the many stories told. What did you enjoy about the author's style?

What difficulties did you have in determining whose story was being told?

How many characters were betrayed by someone else? Which betrayal made you the angriest and why?

What did the science fiction story of "The Blind Assassin" mean to you?

What is meant by the phrase "only the blind are free"?

What redeeming qualities can you find in the male characters?

What qualities in the male characters make you angry?

What positive things can you say about Iris?

What positive things can you say about Laura?

What disappointed you about these two sisters?

See standard questions in the Introduction for more questions.

◇◇◆◇◇

John Ball

In the Heat of the Night

John Ball was born in Schenectady, New York, grew up in Milwaukee, Wisconsin, and attended Carroll College in Waukesha, Wisconsin. He wrote for a number of magazines and newspapers.

Plot summary: In the Southern town of Wells in the Carolinas, the body of orchestra conductor Mantoli is discovered. The conductor was in town to create a music festival for its poor, rural population. The local police arrest a black stranger at the railroad station on suspicion, only to discover he is Virgil Tibbs, a Pasadena homicide investigator. When Tibbs is forced to work side-by-side with the racist chief of police, Bill Gillespie, to solve the murder, more is revealed than just who killed the conductor.

Web site:
none
Reader's guide:
none

Publication date: 1965

Number of pages: 185

Geographic setting: Carolinas, Wells

Time period: 1960s

Series notes: Tibbs is a fish out of water in his first book, but the later titles find him on his more familiar ground in California, until the seventh and final book in the series, where he is in Singapore.

Subject headings: African Americans; Police conduct; Race relations

Appeal points: The eventual triumph over the evils of murder and racism make this book a solid book discussion title in the area of theme. The fact that the author, John Ball, is not an African American can lead to a series of questions dealing with the honesty in the portrayal of Tibbs. Because this book was made into a successful film, the title would also work in discussions of both the book and the film.

Readalikes

Gar Anthony Haywood—similar use of issues regarding race relations

Walter Mosely—similar use of issues regarding race relations

George Pelecanos—similar use of issues regarding race relations

Gary Phillips—similar use of issues regarding race relations

DISCUSSION QUESTIONS

What characteristics of Virgil Tibbs make him a good detective?

Why does Chief Gillespie keep Virgil around when he could have just put him on the next train?

Why does Virgil choose to stay?

Everyone senses a "miasma in the air." What sense of Wells do you get from the book?

If you visited Wells today, what changes would you find?

What could Sam Wood have done to change what happens to him?

How has time changed the central theme of this work?

If Bill Gillespie were still police chief in Wells today, what would he be like?

How does the fact that John Ball is a white man writing about an African American character like Virgil Tibbs affect the theme of this book?

Did the film meet your expectations after reading the novel?

See standard questions in the Introduction for more questions.

◇◇◆◇◇

Sandra Balzo

Uncommon Grounds

Sandra Balzo lives in Brookfield, Wisconsin, with her husband and two children. Sandra spent twenty years in public relations, publicity, and event management before forming her own public relations company, Balzo Communications. She is an active member of the fan mystery community and has worked on many of the Bouchercon: World Mystery Conventions. Her first short story, "The Grass Is Always Greener" (2003) was nominated for an Anthony Award and won the Robert L. Fish Award and a Macavity Award for Best Short Story. Her second story, "Viscery," was an Anthony nominee and won the Derringer Award.

Plot summary: Maggy Thorsen arrives late to the opening of her new coffee store, Uncommon Grounds, only to discover her business partner, Patricia Harper, has been electrocuted by the espresso machine. When the local police begin their investigation, Maggy reluctantly becomes a detective. As she wrestles with the small-town politics in Brookhills, she also begins to develop a romantic interest in one of the detectives.

Publication date: 2004

Number of pages: 244

Geographic setting: Wisconsin, Brookhills

Time period: 2000s

Series notes: This is a stand-alone novel.

Subject heading: Coffee

Appeal points: This novel was nominated for an Anthony and a Macavity Award as the best first novel of the year. Although amateur detectives, who solve their cases in a cozy setting, do not always make the most compelling characters to discuss, this novel should work in a book discussion and will appeal to those who want a gentler read. Discussing this book in a nonlibrary setting, such as the local coffee house, could be an added bonus.

> **Web site:**
> http://www.sandrabalzo.com
> **Reader's guide:**
> http://www.sandrabalzo.com/reading group.html

> **Readalikes**
>
> Donna Andrews—similar use of humor
> Cleo Coyle—similar use of setting
> Dianne Mott Davidson—similar use of food themes
> Joan Hess—similar use of humor

DISCUSSION QUESTIONS

Did this novel teach you anything about coffee or running a coffee house?

What clues do you remember that make this a "play fair" novel?

How good a detective is Maggy?

Maggy refers to her relationship with Sarah as the same as Archie Goodwin and Nero Wolfe. What characteristics do they share?

Do you prefer a first person narrator rather than a third person narration?

What humor did you find in this novel?

Do you think there is a future for Maggy and Pavlik?

What sense of community do you get from the descriptions of Brookhills?

After 9/11, how should society deal with movements like the one discovered in Brookhills?

How bad a man is Gary Donovan?

See standard questions in the Introduction for more questions.

◇◇◆◇◇

Linda Barnes

Deep Pockets

Born and raised in Detroit, Michigan, Linda Barnes attended the Boston University's School of Fine and Applied Arts. After graduating, she taught drama in various Massachusetts schools. Her first mystery novel appeared in 1983 and featured an amateur detective named Michael Spraggue. Her first Carlotta Carlyle novel was published in 1985. Linda lives in Boston with her husband and son.

Plot summary: When an African American Harvard professor named Wilson Chaney is blackmailed over his affair with a student, Denali Brinkman, he hires Private Detective Carlotta Carlyle to stop the threat. Denali was a lonely Native American student, finding solace as a single sculler and eventually illegally moving into the boathouse to avoid her dorm mates. What shocks Carlyle is that Denali committed suicide by immolation, taking the boathouse with her. So the big question becomes who knew about the affair and how did they get Chaney's incriminating letters?

> **Web site:**
> http://www.lindabarnes.com
> **Reader's guide:**
> none

Publication date: 2004
Number of pages: 310
Geographic setting: Masschusetts, Boston
Time period: 2000s
Series notes: Tall, red haired cab-driver and Boston P.I. Carlotta Carlyle, works in a contemporary American society that allows her to stretch her wings as an investigator. Her ward, Paolina, adds complications to her life, as does the occasional man who wanders into her world. There are ten books in the series about Carlotta.

Subject headings: Academia; Race relations

Appeal points: The female private investigator is a major player in contemporary mysteries, so reading about one of these strong, dynamic characters can be fun. This particular book also features the theme of race relations in the United States.

> **Readalikes**
> Sue Grafton's Kinesey Millhone series—similar character
> Jeremiah Healy's John Francis Cuddy series—similar setting
> Sara Paretsky's V. I. Warshawski series—similar character
> Robert B. Parker's Spenser series—similar setting

DISCUSSION QUESTIONS

Did you think of Carlotta as being in a man's world or did you think of a private detective who just happens to be a woman?

What does Carlotta do to get herself defined as a risk taker?

What would make you reject Roz as your backup?

What sense of Harvard University did this novel give you?

What do you think kept Carlotta from attending Harvard?

What does the character of Denali Brinkman mean to you?

What is the worst mistake that Wilson Chaney makes?

Carlotta is dating an African American F.B.I. agent named Leonard Wells. African American Wilson Chaney was sleeping with a Native American girl. Are mixed race relationships doomed to failure in our society? What hope does the text offer?

How smart is Carlotta when it comes to men?

What elements in the ending surprised you?

See standard questions in the Introduction for more questions.

◇◇◆◇◇

Nevada Barr

Track of the Cat

Appropriately, Nevada Barr was born in Nevada and raised in the Sierras. Her first career path was to the theater, and she worked on stage and screen for eighteen years. However, she spent many summers working in the national parks, and it was her interest in the environmental movement that led her to create her series character Anna Pigeon, park ranger.

Plot summary: Assigned to the Guadalupe Mountains to search for mountain lions, Anna Pigeon is unprepared when one of her fellow rangers, Sheila Drury, appears to have been killed by one of the creatures. But Pigeon has suspicions, and when another ranger disappears and she herself is threatened, she knows a more human killer is on the loose.

Web site:
http://www.nevadabarr.com
Reader's guide:
none

Publication date: 1993
Number of pages: 238
Geographic setting: Texas, Guadalupe Mountains National Park
Time period: 1990s
Series notes: Each of the eleven books in this series takes place in a different national park of the United States.
Subject headings: Mountain lion; National parks and reserves—Texas; Park rangers
Appeal points: Pigeon's work situation and attitude about life place her in the category of lone-wolf detective, giving groups plenty to discuss in determining what makes her tick. The unusual setting also leads to a fresh look at the places where death can occur.

Readalikes
Jean Hager—similar use of setting
Tony Hillerman—similar use of setting

DISCUSSION QUESTIONS

What sense of the Guadalupe Mountains National Park did you get from this novel?

What purposes are served by having an animal as the most likely suspect?

Which of Anna's characteristics make her suited for her job in the park?

How do those same characteristics make her suited to be a detective?

Does Anna make the right decisions on this case?

How would you describe the inner spirit of Anna Pigeon?

Anna flees her former life and a death for a new life in the wilderness. Does she save herself?

How should we protect our remaining natural areas?

What aspects of this first novel would entice you to read other books in the series?

See standard questions in the Introduction for more questions.

◇◇◆◇◇

Alice Blanchard

The Breathtaker

Alice Blanchard grew up in Connecticut and studied creative writing and film-making at Emerson and Harvard. She is the author of a collection of short stories, *The Stuntman's Daughter* (University of North Texas, 1996), which won the Katharine Anne Porter Prize. Her novels include *Darkness Peering* (Bantam, 1999) and *Life Sentences* (Warner, 2005). She has also received a PEN Syndicated Fiction Award, a New Literary Award, and a Centrum Artists in Residence Fellowship. She and her husband live in Los Angeles.

Plot summary: Charlie Grover, the sheriff of Promise, Oklahoma, is a single parent with a precocious daughter named Sophie. He is trying to balance his personal problems against the stresses of his job. When a tornado strikes his town, the damage is severe; but things get really creepy when it becomes obvious that three of the victims in the storm were actually murdered. As Charlie begins to discover evidence that a serial killer may be working Tornado Alley, he must turn to storm chasers for help. While a potential relationship with scientist Willa Bellman adds spice to his life, it also forces Charlie to re-establish communication with his storm-chasing father. As Charlie chases across the Plains looking for the right storm to trap his killer, he also races against time to save his family from self-destructing.

Web site:
none
Reader's guide:
none

Publication date: 2003
Number of pages: 391
Geographic setting: Oklahoma, Promise
Time period: 2000s
Series notes: This is a stand-alone novel.
Subject headings: Fathers and daughters; Serial killers; Tornados

Appeal points: This novel is a gripping and fast-paced thriller. The gruesome nature of the killings by a fanatical serial killer does not appeal to all readers, but the strength of the novel is its ability to examine the nature of the characters within the highly stressful situations in which the author places them.

Readalikes

Nevada Barr—similar use of nature as theme

Steve Thayer's *The Weatherman*—similar use of nature as theme

Minette Walters—similar use of psychological suspense

DISCUSSION QUESTIONS

Aside from the tornados, with what sense of place were you left?

In a thriller, the reader needs to be affected. How did the author raise your blood pressure in telling her story?

What things did you learn about tornados that you did not know before you read this book?

In a suspense novel, the characters should be put in danger. What made you worry about the fate of any of the characters in this novel?

Can you defend the statement made by Isaac that Charlie's entire career is really about getting even?

Was Isaac right in keeping the truth from his son?

Why does Charlie not want Sophie to hate her grandfather?

How does Charlie fail as a parent?

How would you keep Sophie away from Boone?

Can you predict the future of Charlie and Willa?

Why do serial killers fascinate us?

See standard questions in the Introduction for more questions.

◇◇◆◇◇

Giles Blunt

Forty Words for Sorrow

Born in North Bay, Canada, Giles Blunt attended Catholic boys' school and then college, where he wrote poetry and an unpublished novel. Upon graduating, he moved to New York City, where he wrote screenplays for such television programs as *Law & Order*, *Street Legal*, and *Night Heat*. He also wrote the novel *Cold Eye* (1989), before launching the John Cardinal series in 2001. Giles lived in New York for twenty-two years, and he met and married his wife Janna there.

Plot summary: John Cardinal is a homicide detective in the very cold region of Algonquin Bay, Canada. A Chippewa teenager named Katie Pine has been missing for months until her body is found in an abandoned mine shaft. This vindicates Cardinal, who had been taken off her case when he insisted she was more than a runaway. As more bodies of young children are discovered, Cardinal and his new partner Lise Delorme find themselves hunting a dangerous serial murderer known as the Windigo Killer. What Cardinal does not know is that his new partner is helping to work an internal affairs investigation against him.

> **Web site:**
> http://www.gilesblunt.com
> **Reader's guide:**
> none

Publication date: 2001

Number of pages: 344

Geographic setting: Canada, Ontario, Algonquin Bay

Time period: 2000s

Series notes: John Cardinal is featured in two more books: *The Delicate Storm* (2003) and *Blackfly Season* (2005).

Subject headings: Children at risk; Mental illness; Police conduct; Serial killers; Winter weather

Appeal points: *Forty Words for Sorrow* won the British Crime Writers' Macallan Silver Dagger Award. This novel should appeal to readers who like their cops to be on the edge. More than a police procedural, this book is also a compelling psychological thriller. The characters' depression is dramatic and disturbing, and the story is greatly enhanced by the setting in the depths of frigid winter weather.

> **Readalikes**
>
> Michael Connelly's Harry Bosch series—similar type of character
>
> Ian Rankin's John Rebus series—similar type of character
>
> John Sandford's Lucas Davenport series—similar serial killer theme

DISCUSSION QUESTIONS

Describe the things you remember about Algonquin Bay.

How did the location affect the story?

Who is most affected by the setting?

What really separates the Ojibwa natives from the rest of the Algonquin residents?

Lise Delorme is also in an alien environment. What factors set her apart from the other police officers?

Which, if any, of Lise's challenges as a woman are her own fault?

What makes John Cardinal a unique individual?

Is his relationship with his wife Catherine believable?

How about his relationship with his daughter Kelly?

Should John be punished for stealing the money he took?

How good a cop is John Cardinal?

What clues did the cops miss during this killing spree?

Were Billy LaBelle's parents justified in writing their letter complaining about the death of Eric?

What turned Eric into the monster he was?

Did you believe him as a character?

Do you like books with the point of view of the killer, or just the point of view of the hunter?

On page 199 (2), Eric says, "[p]eople used to love it, Edie. People still love it. They just won't admit it." Are we not admitting it?

Did you have any sympathy for Edie?

How do you react to her words (p. 196 (3)): "So momentous it had seemed at the time, the murder..."?

What is the theme of this book?

See standard questions in the Introduction for more questions.

◇◇◆◇◇

James Bradley

Wrack

James Bradley was born in Adelaide, South Australia, in 1967. He studied at the University of Adelaide, where he received a law degree, and at the University of South Australia and the Australian Film, Television and Radio School. He has worked as a law clerk, judge's associate, solicitor, research assistant, and editor. Bradley's book of poetry, *Paper Nautilus*, was shortlisted for the National Book Council Award in Australia. He lives in Sydney.

Plot summary: Dr. David Norfolk, archaeologist, has taken on a mission to find evidence of a sixteenth-century Portuguese sailing vessel buried in the sandhills of New South Wales, Australia. He is convinced that his discovery will rewrite Australian history. But instead of the ship, David finds a fifty-year-old corpse of a murdered man. Does the dying man, Kurt Seligman, who lives near the excavation site, hold clues to what happened in the 1930s? Moving between three different time periods, this novel tells the tales of the Portuguese sailors, the university politics that led to a murder, and the obsessive love expressed by the characters in the present. Eventually all seven definitions for the word "wrack" are revealed to the reader through the heartbreaking stories of the characters.

Web site:
none
Reader's guide:
none

Publication date: 1997

Number of pages: 340

Geographic setting: Australia, New South Wales

Time period: 1500s, 1930s, 1940s, 1990s

Series notes: This is a stand-alone novel.

Subject headings: Archaeologists; Excavations; Historical fiction; Shipwrecks

Appeal points: *Wrack* was shortlisted for the Miles Franklin Award and the Commonwealth Writers Prize, and it won the Fellowship of Australian Writers Literature Award and the Kathleen Mitchell Literary Award. This novel appeals to readers who like a thick, rich plot combined with an intense study of obsession and romance. The style of incorporating three different time periods and multiple points of view challenges readers.

Readalikes
Peter Shann Ford's *The Keeper of Dreams*—similar setting and theme
Mardi McConnochie's *Coldwater*—similar setting and theme
Arthur Upfield's Napolean Bonaparte series—similar setting

DISCUSSION QUESTIONS

How would you describe the author's style?

How many points of view were used?

Did the decision not to use quotation marks please you or irritate you?

How does each given definition of "wrack" relate to the novel?

Can you recall particular passages that remain with you after reading this novel?

Claire says both she and David are in the same business, "trying to coax secrets from the dead" (p. 12). Do we admire them for their efforts?

Is David correct in nursing Kurt only to learn about his ship?

Claire warns David (p. 112) to "make sure you hear what's being said, not what you want to hear." Is David a good detective?

Is Claire a more admirable character for wanting to know if Kurt is a murderer?

The author says, "Or maybe the truth is not what lies beneath the sand but the sand itself, always shifting, never certain." Does the novel provide a sense of place?

Is the issue of who discovered Australia an important enough question for people like Fraser, Kurt, and David to sacrifice their lives to the truth?

The text says that "only white men, Europeans, discover." Should Portuguese history define Australian history, or should it be left to the English?

Does Kurt love or obsess?

Does David love or obsess?

Why did Veronica marry Fraser?

Does a mystery novel require a murder?

Is Fraser's death a murder, a case of manslaughter, or a tragic accident?

See standard questions in the Introduction for more questions.

◇◇◆◇◇

Dan Brown

The Da Vinci Code

Dan Brown, the son of a math professor and a musician, is a graduate of Amherst College and Phillips Exeter Academy. Prior to becoming a full-time writer, Brown taught English at Exeter. In 1996 he wrote the techno-thriller *Digital Fortress,* which became a bestselling e-book. His second book, *Deception Point,* was a follow-up, and another techno-thriller. He is married to Blythe Brown, an art historian and painter.

Plot summary: Robert Langdon, an internationally famous symbologist, is hauled out of his hotel bed late one night and rushed to the Louvre. There he discovers the corpse of the museum's curator, Jacques Sauniére, whose body is displayed in a ritualistic manner. Secrets at the site lead Langdon and cryptographer Sophie Neveu, the dead man's granddaughter, to believe that there is a secret society dedicated to an ancient cause, whose members are threatened by death as their membership is exposed. They also discover that Langdon is the number one suspect for Sauniére's murder, and they flee the police, setting off a chase that will cover the continent.

> **Web site:**
> http://www.danbrown.com
>
> **Reader's guide:**
> http://www.danbrown.com/novels/davinci_code/faqs.html or http://www.randomhouse.com/catalog/display.pperl?isbn=9780385504201&view=rg

Publication date: 2003

Number of pages: 454

Geographic setting: England; France; Switzerland

Time period: 2000s

Series notes: The first book to feature Harvard University symbologist Dr. Robert Langdon was *Angels and Demons* (2000). *The Da Vinci Code* is the second in the series.

Subject headings: Conspiracy; Cryptography; Leonardo da Vinci, 1452–1519; Religion

Appeal points: The most remarkable thing about this novel is the inability to put it down until the explanation is given. It is an über-thriller, combining all the elements of adventure, intrigue, and suspense to maintain its audience. Because so many of the "facts" in the novel are controversial, it makes an excellent discussion book. With the release of a major motion picture based on the novel, it will also work for novel-into-film discussion groups.

> **Readalikes**
>
> Ian Caldwell and Dustin Thomason's *The Rule of Four*—similar style of thriller
>
> Ross King's *Ex-Libris*—similar style of thriller
>
> Katherine Neville's *The Eight*—similar style of thriller
>
> Matthew Pearl's *The Dante Club*—similar style of thriller
>
> Arturo Perez-Reverte's *The Flanders Panel*—similar style of thriller

DISCUSSION QUESTIONS

The Da Vinci Code employs brief episodic chapters. Did you enjoy the author's style?

Does *The Da Vinci Code* work best as a play-fair mystery (clues and a puzzle), a novel of suspense (the character[s] are in danger), or a thriller (the reader[s] are thrilled)?

Were you surprised at the revelation of the identity of The Teacher?

Should Robert Langdon have run from the museum with Sophie, or should he have stayed and worked with Fache?

Was the car crash that killed Sophie's parents an accident?

Is Sophie correct in not communicating with her grandfather, Jacques Sauniére, for ten years?

Does this novel read like a nonfiction book with fictional parts or a fiction book with factual information?

To what new concepts were you introduced to while reading this novel?

How did the novel inspire you to seek out the art mentioned in the text?

Why would it be difficult to keep a secret as long as this one was kept?

If the Holy Grail had been revealed, in what ways would it have changed the world? Would you have revealed the Holy Grail?

In what ways did *The Da Vinci Code* change your way of thinking about your faith? Can religion and science coexist?

See standard questions in the Introduction for more questions.

◇◇◆◇◇

Ken Bruen

The Guards

Ken Bruen was born in 1951 in Galway, Ireland. As a teenager, he was accepted into acting school at London's Royal Academy of Dramatic Art. After turning to teaching, Bruen earned an M.A. and then began to travel and teach foreign students. At age twenty-eight, he was arrested in Rio de Janeiro when a bar fight broke out. He was jailed, tortured, and raped in prison, then released after four months without being charged. For three years Bruen was unable to function, but he eventually regained his self-esteem by teaching children with learning disabilities. He earned a degree in metaphysics as he struggled to understand the evil that had happened to him in South America. Turning to crime writing, which he loved to read, he created the cop character Brandt for *A White Arrest* (1998), *Taming the Alien* (2000), *The McDead* (2002), *Blitz* (2002), and *Vixen* (2003). His nonseries novels include *Rilke on Black* (1997), *The Hackman Blues* (1997), *Her Last Call to Louis Macniece* (1997), *London Boulevard* (2001), and *Dispatching Baudelaire* (2004).

Plot summary: Ann Henderson thought her sixteen-year-old daughter, Sarah, had committed suicide until a man called to say, "She was drowned." So Ann hires ex-Garda Jack Taylor, an unofficial investigator, or finder of things. Ireland has no P.I.s, but Jack has some problems even in his unofficial capacity because he is a raging, poetic, lamenting drunk. He also associates with a melancholy singer named Catherine B. and partners with a dangerous psycho named Sutton. Catherine gives Jack the clue he needs to look at Bartholomew Planter, a rich man with an interest in young women. There will be tragic occurrences before this case is resolved, and people will not walk away whole.

> **Web site:**
> http://www.kenbruen.com
> **Reader's guide:**
> none

Publication date: 2001
Number of pages: 291
Geographic setting: Ireland, Galway
Time period: 1990s
Series notes: *The Guards* has been followed by *The Killing of the Tinkers* (2002), *The Magdelen Martyrs* (2003), *The Dramatist* (2004), and *Priest* (2006).
Subject headings: Alcohol; Children at risk
Appeal points: This is one of those novels that either appeals to a reader or it is rejected out of hand. At times the novel reads like poetry, not only in its use of language but also in its structure. Poetic or not, this is a tough, nearly noir novel with a hopeless downward spiral. What saves it from its own despair is the ironic appeal of its antihero main character.

> **Readalikes**
>
> Lawrence Block's Matthew Scudder series—similar use of alcoholism as a theme
> Bartholomew Gill's Peter McGarr series—similar use of setting

DISCUSSION QUESTIONS

What did the author's style do for you?

When the doctor asks Jack "for what" Jack should be saved (p. 95), what should the answer be?

How would you describe Jack's memories of his father? His mother?

Why does Cathy tell Jack about her father's death (p. 50)?

What attracts Ann to Jack?

How "instrumental" is Jack regarding Brendan Flood's confession?

Why does Sarah kill herself?

How important is it to know the authors that Jack is reading?

Mrs. Bailey says Jack is a "good man" who doesn't know he is—so, is he?

Does Jack make the right decision at the end of the book?

See standard questions in the Introduction for more questions.

◇◇◆◇◇

James Lee Burke

Cimarron Rose

James Lee Burke was born in 1936 in Houston, Texas, the son of an engineer and a homemaker. Burke attended the University of Southwest Louisiana, but earned both his B.A. and M.A. from the University of Missouri. He worked as a surveyor, a social worker, a newspaper reporter, and an English professor while moving around the country. In 1960 he married his wife Pearl; they have four children. One daughter, Alafair Burke, has joined her father in the ranks of published crime novelists. Early in his writing career, he wrote *Half of Paradise* (1965), *To the Bright and Shining Sun* (1970), *Lay Down My Sword and Shield* (1971), *Two for Texas* (1982), and *The Convict* (1985). After being rejected 111 times, his next novel, *The Lost Get-Back Boogie*, was published in 1986 and nominated for a Pulitzer Prize. He then began his series of crime novels featuring Dave Robicheaux, including *The Neon Rain* (1987), *Heaven's Prisoners* (1988—filmed as a major motion picture), *Black Cherry Blues* (1989—Edgar Award for Best Novel), *A Morning for Flamingos* (1990), *A Stained White Radiance* (1992), *In the Electric Mist with Confederate Dead* (1993), *Dixie City Jam* (1994), *Burning Angel* (1995), *Cadillac Jukebox* (1996), *Sunset Limited* (1998), *Purple Cane Road* (2000), *Jolie Blon's Bounce* (2002—nominations for the Edgar Award and the Hammett Prize), *Last Car to Elysian Fields* (2003), and *Crusader's Cross* (2005). His nonseries book is *White Doves at Morning* (2002). He lives alternately in New Iberia, Louisiana, and Missoula, Montana.

Plot summary: Lawyer Billy Bob Holland is a former Texas Ranger with a violent past that he desperately tries to suppress. When he is forced by circumstances to defend his own illegitimate son, Lucas Smothers, against a charge of rape and murder, he must confront a series of ghosts from his past. He finds himself aligned against elements of the small town of Deaf Smith including the cops, some unruly teens, and one dangerous psycho. As he takes on this battle, he finds aid from a female cop who may also be out to bust him on a drug deal. Billy Bob struggles to deal with his violent nature while trying to be the mythical hero this town needs.

> **Web site:**
> http://www.jamesleeburke.com
> **Reader's guide:**
> none

Publication date: 1997
Number of pages: 288
Geographic setting: Texas, Deaf Smith
Time period: 1990s
Series notes: This is the first novel in a series that includes *Heartwood* (1999), *Bitterroot* (2001), and *In the Moon of Red Ponies* (2004).

> **Readalikes**
>
> James Crumley—similar style of character
>
> Charles Todd's Ian Rutledge series—similar use of a haunted character

Subject headings: Courtroom dramas; Lawyers; The West

Appeal points: This novel won the Edgar Award for Best Novel. Burke is famous for being a poetical writer. The trick to his appeal is whether a reader can balance the extreme violence that is generated by his characters with his lyrical prose.

DISCUSSION QUESTIONS

How would you describe Burke's writing style?

Are there any particular passages you remember from this novel?

How would you describe Billy Bob: hero or villain?

Does Billy Bob have faith in anything?

Do you believe that a person can be haunted by the past as Billy Bob has been?

What role does the Rose of Cimarron play in this novel? How crucial is Sam in the development of Billy Bob?

How should Billy Bob have dealt with Vernon Smothers regarding his son Lucas?

How good a father is Billy Bob before and after this tragedy?

Does Billy Bob's relationship with Pete redeem him as a character?

What attracts a woman like Mary Beth to a man like Billy Bob?

Is Billy Bob a violent man by nature, or is he forced to be violent by circumstances out of his control?

See standard questions in the Introduction for more questions.

◇◇◆◇◇

Jan Burke

Bones

Born in 1953 in Houston, Texas, Jan (Fischer) Burke has a B.A. in history from California State University—Long Beach. Besides her Irene Kelly novels, she wrote the thriller *Nine* (2002). Burke received the Macavity Award for her short story "Unharmed" and the Agatha Award for her short story "The Man in the Civil Suit." In 1988 she married musician Timothy Burke. They live in California with their two dogs, Cappy and Britches.

Plot summary: Irene Kelly covered the disappearance of Julia Sayre, a young mother of two. For four years, the reporter has been reminded that she failed, and the only person who really knows what happened is on death row. When Nick Parrish decides to talk, he gains his temporary freedom by leading an expedition into the Sierra Nevada to find the bodies. Irene goes along and becomes a victim of the revenge sought by this desperate killer.

Web site:
http://www.janburke.com
Reader's guide:
none

Publication date: 1999

Number of pages: 378

Geographic setting: California, Las Piernas; California, Sierra Nevadas

Time period: 1990s

Series notes: Burke's Irene Kelly series includes *Goodnight, Irene* (1993), *Sweet Dreams, Irene* (1994), *Dear Irene* (1995), *Remember Me, Irene* (1996), *Hocus* (1997), *Liar* (1998), *Flight* (2001—a novel starring Irene's husband Frank Harriman), and *Bloodlines* (2005).

Subject headings: Death-row inmates; Journalists; Serial killers; Sierra Nevadas

Appeal points: *Bones* was nominated for the Anthony Award and won the Edgar Award for Best Novel of 1999. This novel is a suspenseful thriller that has a high level of tension.

Readalikes

Barbara D'Amato's Cat Marsala series—similar use of a journalist detective

Thomas Harris' Hannibal Lechter series—similar serial killer theme

Carolyn G. Hart's *Letter from Home*—similar use of a journalist detective

Val McDermid's Lindsay Gordon series—similar use of a journalist detective

DISCUSSION QUESTIONS

How driven should journalists become about a story they cover?

How long should inmates stay on death row before their execution?

Is the truth important enough in this case to forgive what happens when Parrish is released?

Why is Parrish so obsessed with Irene?

Should the authorities have agreed to the deal with Parrish?

Is the motivation enough in this novel to change a person into "The Moth"?

How should we feel about criminals when we see the root cause of their crimes exposed?

See standard questions in the Introduction for more questions.

◇◇◆◇◇

James M. Cain

James M. Cain was born in 1892 in Annapolis, Maryland. He earned a B.A. from Washington College in 1910 and an M.A. in 1917. From 1918 through 1919, Cain served with the U.S. Army in the American Expeditionary Forces. Cain worked as a journalist from 1917 to 1931 and as a Hollywood screenwriter from 1932 until 1948. His other novels are *Serenade* (1937), *Mildred Pierce* (1941), *Love's Lovely Counterfeit* (1942), *The Embezzler* (1944), *Past All Dishonor* (1946), *The Butterfly* (1947), *The Sinful Woman* (1947), *The Moth* (1948), *Jealous Woman* (1950), *Galatea* (1953), *The Root of His Evil* (1954), *Mignon* (1962), *The Magician's Wife* (1965), *Rainbow's End* (1975), *The Institute* (1976), and *Cloud Nine* (1984). Cain married four times. In 1947 he moved back to Maryland, where he died of a heart attack in 1977. He was selected a Grand Master by the Mystery Writers of America in 1970.

> **Web site:**
> none

Double Indemnity

Plot summary: Insurance salesman Walter Huff stops by the Nirdlinger household to update the policy of Mr. Nirdlinger. When Mrs. Phyllis Nirdlinger asks about the double indemnity clause in the policy, Huff knows he should run. Instead he falls in lust with her. Now, the two head down a dark path together, beginning to plot a way to get rid of Mr. Nirdlinger.

> **Reader's guide:**
> none

Publication date: 1935

Number of pages: 107

Geographic setting: California, Glendale

Time period: 1930s

Series notes: This is a stand-alone novel.

Subject headings: Adultery; Insurance fraud

Appeal points: This novel can be used in a novel-into-film discussion. Raymond Chandler (see entry under Raymond Chandler) received an Academy Award nomination for the screenplay *Double Indemnity*. Readers who need a hero do not typically enjoy this novel. The idea that love leads to death is a powerful theme but may not be enjoyed by all readers.

> **Readalikes**
>
> David Ellis' *Line of Vision*—similar use of obsessive love
>
> Cornell Woolrich—similar use of suspense

DISCUSSION QUESTIONS

Why does Walter fall in love with Phyllis?

What causes Walter to shift his affections to Lola?

Is Walter able to love anyone?

How would you describe Walter's relationship with Keys?

Why does Walter try to embezzle from a company that respects him?

Which is the greater motivator: sex or greed?

What makes the characters in this novel believable?

Which characters would you describe as amoral or immoral?

How culpable is the insurance company in this murder?

Does the final resolution of Walter and Phyllis' relationship serve justice?

See standard questions in the Introduction for more questions.

◇◇◆◇◇

The Postman Always Rings Twice

Reader's guide:
none

Readalikes

David Ellis' *Line of Vision*—similar use of obsessive love

Cornell Woolrich—similar use of suspense

Plot summary: When Frank Chambers drifts into Nick Papadakis' Twin Oaks Tavern, he gets more than a good meal. He falls into a relationship with Cora, the owner's wife. As the couple's affair progresses, the relationship becomes fatal for Frank.

Publication date: 1934

Number of pages: 103

Geographic setting: California

Time period: 1930s

Series notes: This is a stand-alone novel.

Subject heading: Adultery

Appeal points: This novel can be used in a novel-into-film discussion. Readers who need a hero do not generally enjoy this novel. Although not enjoyed by all readers, the idea that love leads to death is a powerful theme and makes for great discussion.

DISCUSSION QUESTIONS

What would Frank's fate be if he had never met Cora?

What effect has the Depression had on Frank's development?

What does Cora mean when she talks about Nick's "greasiness"?

Are Frank and Cora in love?

How would you define Frank and Cora's love?

Is Cora's reason for leaving Nick justifiable?

Which is the greater motivator: sex or greed?

Does Cora's death avenge Nick?

How many things happen "twice" in this novel?

Why does Frank tell us this story?

Is it irony or justice that Frank is punished for a crime he did not commit?

See standard questions in the Introduction for more questions.

◇◇◆◇◇

Raymond Chandler

Raymond Chandler was born in 1888 in Chicago, Illinois. When his parents divorced, he moved with his mother to England, where he was educated at Dulwich College preparatory school. From 1908 to 1912, Chandler worked as a reporter in England. From 1912 to 1917, he was an accountant in a sporting goods store in Los Angeles. He served in the Canadian Army from 1917 to 1918 and then in the Canadian Royal Air Force from 1918 until 1919. From 1922 until 1932, he worked for the Dabney Oil Syndicate, moving from bookkeeper to auditor to vice president. Chandler married Pearl Cecily Hurlburt in 1924; they were married for thirty years until her death in 1954. Chandler's writing career began after he was laid off from the oil company at age forty-four. His first crime short story was published in 1933 and his stories have been collected in numerous editions. All of his novels feature the compelling character Philip Marlowe, private investigator. In addition to writing novels, Chandler worked with the studios as a screenwriter beginning in 1943. Chandler received an Academy Award nomination for the screenplay *Double Indemnity* (see entry under James M. Cain). He received an Edgar and an Oscar nomination for the screenplay *The Blue Dahlia*. Chandler died in La Jolla, California, in 1959.

Series notes: *The Big Sleep* is the first novel in the series. It is followed by *Farewell, My Lovely* (1940), *The High Window* (1942), *The Lady in the Lake* (1943), *The Little Sister* (1949), *The Long Goodbye* (1953—Edgar Award winner as best novel), *Playback* (1958), and *Poodle Springs* (1989—completed by Robert B. Parker).

Web site:
none

The Big Sleep

Plot summary: Los Angeles private detective Philip Marlowe is hired by General Sternwood to collect the gambling debts of his eldest daughter, Vivian, from a hood named Eddie Mars who may be blackmailing the family. Everyone, including the youngest daughter Carmen, believes Marlowe has been hired to locate Rusty Regan, the missing husband of Vivian. As the P.I. tries to accomplish the first task, he finds himself drawn into a corrupt world of pornography, gambling, and murder that inevitably leads to an attempt to explain who killed Rusty.

Readers' guide:
none

Publication date: 1939
Number of pages: 175
Geographic setting: California, Los Angeles
Time period: 1930s
Subject headings: Gambling; Pornography

Appeal points: This novel works well in a novel-into-film discussion. The 1946 version with Humphrey Bogart and Lauren Bacall was followed by a 1977 film with Robert Mitchum in the role of Marlowe. The character of Marlowe is the classic private detective as knight errant, a man who for a small fee will be fiercely loyal to his client and battle all the evils of a corrupt world.

Readalikes

Michael Connelly's Harry Bosch series—similar style of character

Dashiell Hammett's *The Maltese Falcon*—similar style of private eye novel

---

DISCUSSION QUESTIONS

How much personal information did you learn about Philip Marlowe?

When Marlowe sees the black knight he says, "I would sooner or later have to climb up there and help him." What does this tell us about his personality?

Can you describe this private eye's code of conduct?

What distinguishes the two sisters in this novel?

Why does the General like his bootlegging son-in-law Rusty?

Why does Marlowe like the General, considering that Marlowe says, "To hell with the rich. They made me sick"?

Why does Marlowe tear apart his bed after Carmen's visit?

What purpose is served by the description of Carmen's "little sharp predatory teeth"?

Why does Chandler make Marlowe a cynical wisecracking man?

Is Marlowe a romantic idealist?

How did the author use language to propel his story?

What descriptions of Los Angeles can you remember from this work?

How corrupt is this Los Angeles in comparison to today's version?

Chandler has been accused of being both a misogynist and a chauvinist. What evidence for this do you see in this work?

See standard questions in the Introduction for more questions.

◇◇◆◇◇

The Long Goodbye

Reader's guide:
http://www.randomhouse.com/catalog/
display.pperl?isbn=9780394757681
&view=rg

Plot summary: Late one night Marlowe rescues a man named Terry Lennox who has been dumped outside a bar while in an alcoholic stupor. A damaged veteran, Lennox, who could be accused of murdering his wealthy wife, uses Marlowe to escape to Mexico. Once across the border, Lennox commits suicide, and the investigation ends. Later, Marlowe is hired to rescue the self-pitying author Roger Wade from his alcohol-fueled self-destruction, a task at which Marlowe fails. Each of these murders draws Marlowe into a world of corruption and lies, and leads to an examination of the characters that may raise issues about the author Raymond Chandler's own history.

Publication date: 1953

Number of pages: 315

Geographic setting: California, Los Angeles

Time period: 1950s

Subject headings: Authors; Suicide

Appeal points: *The Long Goodbye* won the Edgar Award as best novel. This novel would work as a novel-into-film discussion title especially because the Robert Altman film made in 1973 is a startling diversion from the Chandler canon. The character of Roger Wade in this novel may echo many of Raymond Chandler's personal demons and therefore there is an added dimension to reading this work. This novel also works as a male-bonding tale and should appeal to male readers.

Readalikes

James Crumley—similar use of thematic device

Dashiell Hammett's *The Maltese Falcon*—similar style of private eye novel

DISCUSSION QUESTIONS

Does Marlowe's code restore order to the chaos in this novel, or is it an anachronism?

Is Harlan Potter evil because he is rich? Can money buy happiness, or is Marlowe right when he says, "You've got a hundred million dollars and all it has bought you is a pain in the neck"?

Chandler has been accused of being both a misogynist and a chauvinist. What evidence for this do you see in this work?

Chandler had a problem with alcohol. What role does alcohol play in this novel and what message do you think the author was trying to send?

How much of Wade's speeches about writing can be attributed to Chandler's own feelings about his writings?

How melancholy is the relationship between Terry and Marlowe?

Is Marlowe betrayed by Terry?

Is justice served with the death of Eileen Wade?

See standard questions in the Introduction for more questions.

◇◇◆◇◇

Agatha Christie

The Murder of Roger Ackroyd

Agatha Miller was born in Torquay, Devon, England, in 1890. She married Colonel Archibald Christie in 1914, and they had one daughter. They divorced in 1928. In 1930, she married Sir Max Mallowan. Over her career, Christie wrote more than ninety novels and plays, including the longest continuous running play in theater history, *The Mousetrap.* Her first novel, *The Mysterious Affair at Styles,* introduced detective Hercule Poirot. Her other main series character is Jane Marple. Christie also wrote romantic suspense under the name Mary Westmacott. In 1954 she was made a Grand Master by the Mystery Writers of America; and she received the Order of Dame Commander of the British Empire in 1971. She died in 1976.

Web site:
http://uk.agathachristie
.com/site/home
Reader's guide:
none

Plot summary: In the village of King's Abbot, rumors are flying that some recent deaths may be murder. Mrs. Ferrars has put off Roger Ackroyd for one year while she mourns her dead husband, and then she is found dead, a suicide. Shortly after, Ackroyd is found murdered. When Poirot arrives to investigate, his case will become one of the classics of mystery fiction, featuring one of the greatest and most controversial endings in mystery fiction history.

Publication date: 1926
Number of pages: 213
Geographic setting: England, King's Abbot
Time period: 1920s

Readalikes

Arthur Conan Doyle's Sherlock Holmes stories—similar use of the Great Thinking Detective

Dorothy L. Sayers' Lord Peter Wimsey series—similar use of plots

Series notes: There are forty-one volumes in the Hercule Poirot canon of which this book is number four.

Subject heading: Suicide

Appeal points: The powerful appeal of the retired Belgian detective Hercule Poirot cannot be underestimated. Although odd, he is a great detective. Christie writes in the style of the classic Golden Age mysteries, so modern readers will have to make accommodations for pacing and characters.

DISCUSSION QUESTIONS

What is the appeal of Hercule Poirot to generations of readers?

What separates Hercule from Sherlock Holmes?

Why do you think Christie made Poirot a foreigner to England?

Does Mrs. Ferrars deserve her fate?

Does Roger Ackroyd deserve his fate?

Did the revelation of the murderer surprise you?

Did Agatha Christie "play fair"?

See standard questions in the Introduction for more questions.

◇◇◆◇◇

Robert Clark

Mr. White's Confession

Robert Clark was born in 1952 in St. Paul, Minnesota. He is the author of the novel *In the Deep Midwinter* (1997), and the nonfiction books *River of the West* (1995) and *The Solace of Food: A Life of James Beard* (1993). He lives in Seattle with his wife and two children.

Web site:
none

Reader's guide:
http://www.readinggroupguides
.com/guides/mr_whites_
confession.asp

Plot summary: Herbert White, an odd fellow, records the minutiae of his life in notebooks and romances Hollywood starlets from a distance. A loner who loves photography, he amuses himself by taking pictures of the "taxi dancers" from the Aragon Ballroom. Then, Charlene Mortensen, one of the girls, is found strangled. One month later, when Herbert's special friend Ruby Fahey is found murdered, Lieutenant Wesley Horner arrests Herbert. It seems like an easy case for the police, until Horner realizes Herbert's confession is not right. Herbert can only remember the distant past.

Publication date: 1998
Number of pages: 341
Geographic setting: Minnesota, St. Paul
Time period: 1930s, 1940s

Readalikes

George Dawes Green's *The Caveman's Valentine*—similar use of challenged individuals

Laurie King's *To Play the Fool*—similar use of challenged individuals

Series notes: This is a stand-alone novel.
Subject headings: Amnesia; Memory loss
Appeal points: This novel won the Edgar Award for best novel of the year. The contrast of Wesley's hard-boiled life with the Victorian innocence of Mr. White appeals to readers who like to be challenged. This is a powerful historical novel with its depiction of Depression-age America.

DISCUSSION QUESTIONS

What is special about reading a book with an unreliable narrator?

How were you affected by the journals of Herbert White?

What should society do with a man like Herbert?

How innocent is Herbert?

How capable of love is Herbert?

What role does Ruby play in this story?

What role does Veronica Galvin play in this story?

Is Wesley a good cop?

What role does Maggie play in this story?

Should Wesley have sent the letter to the governor?

Why does Mr. White confess?

Who is good in the book, and who is evil?

See standard questions in the Introduction for more questions.

◇◇◆◇◇

Max Allan Collins

True Detective

Max Allan Collins, Jr., was born in Muscatine, Iowa, in 1948. Collins has an A.A. degree from Muscatine Community College and a B.A. and M.F.A. from the University of Iowa. Collins is a Renaissance man, as he has established impressive credentials in numerous artistic fields, including writing, music, and film. Besides his Nate Heller series, he has other series characters in Eliot Ness, Quarry, and Mallory. The author of a continuing series of mysteries based on great disasters, he also scripted the Dick Tracy comic strip for fourteen years. He has created many memorable comic book characters such as Ms. Tree, Mike Danger, and a new version of Johnny Dynamite. His graphic novel, *The Road to Perdition*, was made into a major motion picture starring Tom Hanks and Paul Newman. He has written many movie tie-in novels for Hollywood, and he has written, produced, and directed his own independent films. Collins has also written numerous nonfiction works including studies of Mickey Spillane, pin-up girl art, and a history of mystery fiction. A musician, he performs in two different bands. As a playwright, Collins received a 2005 Edgar Award nomination for *Eliot Ness: An Untouchable Life*. He is married to mystery writer Barbara Collins, and they have one son named Nate. He lives in Muscatine.

Web site:
http://maxallancollins.com
Reader's guide:
none

Plot summary: As a young cop, Nate Heller accidentally gets involved in the attempted assassination of Frank Nitti, Al Capone's replacement. He resigns from the police force in disgust, which wins him the admiration of pal Eliot Ness. Heller opens his A-1 Detective Agency and is hired by Capone to protect Chicago Mayor Cermak from an assassination plot. A second client, a beautiful actress, hires him to find her brother. All three cases wrap around each other, with many famous faces appearing. Eventually Heller's hunt for the killer of Jake Lingle, a Chicago reporter, gets the reader to the climax of this tale.

Publication date: 1983
Number of pages: 358

Readalikes

Steve Monroe—similar use of historical period and setting

Kris Nelscott's Smokey Dalton series—similar use of setting and genre

Geographic setting: Illinois, Chicago
Time period: 1930s
Series notes: This is the first book in a series that includes *True Crime* (1984), *The Million-Dollar Wound* (1986), *Neon Mirage* (1988), *Stolen Away* (1991—Shamus Award for Best Private Eye Novel of the Year), *Carnal Hours* (1994), *Blood and Thunder* (1995), *Damned in Paradise*

(1996), *Flying Blind* (1998), *Majic Man* (1999), *Angel in Black* (2001), and *Chicago Confidential* (2002).

     Subject headings: Capone, Al; Cermak, Anton; Gangsters; Lingle, Jake; Nitti, Frank

     Appeal points: This novel won the Shamus Award as the best private eye novel of the year (see entry in series above).

DISCUSSION QUESTIONS

What is your reaction to the use of real historical figures as characters in a fiction book?

Why do you think Collins made Heller half-Jewish and half-Irish?

How should Nate handle the memory of his father's death?

How noble a knight is Nate?

How ethical is it for Nate to work for Nitti?

Did Collins develop a convincing explanation to this historical mystery?

See standard questions in the Introduction for more questions.

◇◇◆◇◇

Michael Connelly

Michael Connelly was born in 1956. While attending the University of Florida at Gainesville, he discovered the novels of Raymond Chandler. In 1980, he grad-

Web site:
http://www.michaelconnelly.com/
index.html

uated with a major in journalism and a minor in creative writing. Subsequently, Connelly worked as a newspaper reporter in Florida and in Los Angeles. Along with his two cowriters, Connelly became a Pulitzer Prize finalist for feature writing for an article they wrote about the survivors of an airplane crash. He is now a full-time novelist. He lives with his wife and children in Florida.

Series notes: Connelly has suggested that eventually all of his novels are going to be tied together in one literary arc. In addition to this novel, his other

Reader's guide:
none

works are *The Black Ice* (1993—Harry Bosch), *The Concrete Blonde* (1994—Harry Bosch), *The Last Coyote* (1995—Harry Bosch), *The Poet* (1996—Jack McEvoy—winner of the Anthony Award), *Trunk Music* (1997—Harry Bosch), *Blood Work* (1998—Terry McCaleb—Anthony Award for Best Novel), *Angels Flight* (1999—Harry Bosch), *Void Moon* (1999—Cassie Black), *A Darkness More Than Night* (2001—Harry Bosch & Terry McCaleb), *Chasing the Dime* (2002—a stand-alone novel), *City of Bones* (2002—Harry Bosch—nominated for an Edgar and winner of the Anthony Award for Best Novel), *Lost Light* (2003—Harry Bosch), *The Narrows* (2004—Harry Bosch), *The Closers* (2005—Harry Bosch), and *The Lincoln Lawyer* (2005—Mickey Haller, Harry's half-brother).

The Black Echo

Plot summary: L.A. homicide detective Hieronymous (Harry) Bosch is called to Mulholland Dam when an anonymous tip reveals a dead body hidden in a drainpipe. When Harry recognizes the victim as a fellow Vietnam tunnel rat Billy Meadows, it leads him to persevere in his investigation when the department would just write the death off as another drug-related incident. As Harry reveals a crucial connection to a major crime, it forces him to cooperate with the F.B.I. but also attracts the attention of the internal affairs officers of the L.A.P.D.

Readalikes

Raymond Chandler's Philip Marlowe series—similar use of setting and character

Ian Rankin's John Rebus series—similar use of character

Publication date: 1992
Number of pages: 375
Geographic setting: California, Los Angeles
Time period: 1990s

Subject headings: Bank robbery; F.B.I.; Police conduct; Tunnels; Vietnamese Conflict, 1961–1975

Appeal points: This novel won the Edgar Award as the best first novel of the year and was nominated for an Anthony Award. Bosch is one of those antiheroes who garner a reader's respect. The way that Connelly uses the Los Angeles landscape is reminiscent of his literary idol, Raymond Chandler.

DISCUSSION QUESTIONS

What does the author do to project an image of Los Angeles on the pages of this novel?

Can Vietnam be blamed for the crime in this novel?

What sends Harry to the police force while Billy ends up dead in a tunnel?

Does Bosch bring his problems on himself?

If you were Jerry, how would you deal with Harry as your partner?

How vulnerable is Bosch to a woman like Eleanor?

Is Bosch a hero?

How big a betrayal is the climax of this novel?

See standard questions in the Introduction for more questions.

◇◇◆◇◇

Blood Work

Plot summary: Since his retirement from the F.B.I., all Terry McCaleb wants to do is live out a quiet life on his boat, protecting the new heart that beats in his chest since his surgery. But when Graciela Rivers taps him on the chest one day, telling him her dead sister Gloria's heart is now his, he is forced to begin an investigation into the real cause of Gloria's death.

Publication date: 1998

Number of pages: 391

Geographic setting: California, Los Angeles

Time period: 1990s

Subject headings: Heart transplants; Serial killers

Appeal factors: This novel won the Macavity and Anthony awards and was nominated for the Edgar and the Barry. The book works well for novel-into-film discussion groups. What more

> **Readalikes**
>
> Tess Gerritsen's *Body Double*—similar use of thriller
>
> Jane Haddam's Gregor Demarkian series—similar use of character in a thriller setting

compelling drama can be established in the reader's mind than the search for the killer of the donor of the heart beating in the detective's chest?

DISCUSSION QUESTIONS

Is it heroic or stupid for Terry to take on this quest?

Why does Terry need to be an investigator?

Why can Terry not let go from an investigation?

What characteristics does Terry share with a serial killer?

What role does Raymond serve in this novel?

Did Terry's attraction to Graciela add to the story or detract?

See standard questions in the Introduction for more questions.

◇◦◄►◦◇

The Poet

Plot summary: After homicide detective Sean McEvoy commits suicide, he is found dead in his car with an Edgar Allan Poe quote written in his own handwriting. Convinced that his twin brother would not commit suicide, Denver reporter Jack McEvoy decides to investigate. When he discovers that other cops have died with the same cryptic notes appearing at the crime scene, the F.B.I.'s Behavioral Science Section sends Rachel Walling to work side by side with Jack.

> **Publication date:** 1996
> **Number of pages:** 435
> **Geographic setting:** Colorado, Denver
> **Time period:** 1990s

Subject headings: Journalists; Pedophilia; Serial killers

Appeal factors: This novel was nominated for the Hammett Award and won the Anthony Award as the best novel of the year. It works as a thriller, and its big appeal is the chase to find the killer. Reading about a serial killer and pedophilia may not be to the taste of all readers.

Readalikes
Thomas Harris' Hannibal Lechter series—similar serial killer theme
Mary Willis Walker's *The Red Scream*—similar serial killer theme

DISCUSSION QUESTIONS

What really motivates Jack to hunt for his brother's killer?

How does the author make it believable that a reporter would be trusted by the F.B.I.?

Did the romantic subplot add to or detract from the story?

Has the Internet made it easier for the bad guys?

Why are we so fascinated by serial killers?

What should society do with a pedophile like William Gladden?

How did the author surprise you at the end of the story?

See standard questions in the Introduction for more questions.

◇◇◀▶◇◇

Thomas H. Cook

Thomas H. Cook was born in 1947 in Fort Payne, Alabama. He received degrees in English and philosophy from Georgia State College (1969) and graduate degrees in American history from Hunter College, City University of New York (1972), and Columbia University (1976). While attending school, he supported himself in a variety of jobs, from advertising executive for U.S. Industrial Chemicals to clerk-typist for the Association for Help of Retarded Adults. He taught English and history at DeKalb Community College in Clarkson, Georgia, for three years before deciding—upon publication of his first book—to become a full-time writer. Cook is the author of over twenty books, including two works of true crime. His novels have been nominated for the Edgar Allan Poe Award, the Macavity Award, and the Dashiell Hammett Prize. He lives in New York City and on Cape Cod.

> **Web site:**
> none

> **Reader's guide:**
> none

> **Readalikes**
>
> Margaret Atwood's *The Blind Assassin*—similar unreliable narrator
>
> Jim Fergus' *The Wild Girl: The Notebooks of Ned Giles, 1932*—similar use of the theme of guilt
>
> David Guterson's *Snow Falling on Cedars*—similar unreliable narrator and use of guilt as a theme
>
> Carolyn G. Hart's *Letter from Home*—similar style of plot
>
> William Hefferman's *Beulah Hill*—similar setting
>
> Harper Lee's *To Kill a Mockingbird*—similar setting and theme

Breakheart Hill

Plot summary: Kelli Troy bravely writes an essay about "the race problem" for her high-school newspaper, edited by Ben Wade. As upset as this makes the community in 1962, no one anticipates that she will suffer for her honesty, let alone be murdered. Local ruffian Lyle Gates is tried and convicted for the deed, and the community tries to forget. Years later, Dr. Ben Wade is helping Kelli's mother close her estate. This small act opens a floodgate of memories that makes the doctor explain the real reasons for what happened and his culpability in it.

Publication date: 1995
Number of pages: 264
Geographic setting: Alabama, Choctaw
Time period: 1960s, 1990s
Series notes: This is a stand-alone novel.
Subject headings: African Americans; Race relations; The South
Appeal points: This novel was nominated for the Hammett Award. Though difficult to read because of the way it plays with time and because of the unreliable nature of the narrator, its powerful theme that one thoughtless act can cause immeasurable harm is very moving.

DISCUSSION QUESTIONS

How did you enjoy the author's style, especially his use of time?

Why is Kelli incapable of reciprocating Ben's love?

What separates Kelli from the rest of the residents of Choctaw?

How could Kelli have changed her effect on Mary Diehl?

What role does Luke play in this story?

Why is Lyle so upset when Kelli refuses to respond to his insults at Cuffy's café?

Is Lyle Gates an anomaly, or does he represent all of Choctaw?

Why can race relations not improve in this town?

Should Dr. Ben Wade be the person whom the community relies on to heal itself?

Why did the Sheriff fail to seek the truth?

How culpable is Ben in the events that took place in Choctaw?

What is the meaning of the opening sentence of the book, "This is the darkest story I've ever heard."?

See standard questions in the Introduction for more questions.

◇◇◆◇◇

The Chatham School Affair

Plot summary: This novel represents the memories of attorney Henry Griswald who carries the guilt over actions taken in 1926. Henry's father was headmaster of Chatham School when he hired Elizabeth Channing to teach art there. The emotional impact she has on the boys and on one teacher, Leland Reed, leads to a series of tragic events and deaths. As the story is slowly revealed incident by incident, the reader discovers who may be responsible for the actions that occurred on Black Pond so many years ago.

> **Reader's guide:**
> none

Publication date: 1996
Number of pages: 292
Geographic setting: Massachusetts, Cape Cod, Chatham
Time period: 1920s
Series notes: This is a stand-alone novel.
Subject headings: Academia; Love affairs; Private schools
Appeal points: *The Chatham School Affair* won the Edgar Allan Poe Award for Best Novel in 1996. It is a story about people wracked with guilt,

Readalikes

Margaret Atwood's *The Blind Assassin*—similar unreliable narrator

David Guterson's *Snow Falling on Cedars*—similar unreliable narrator and use of guilt as a theme

Anthony Pyper's *The Lost Girls*—similar setting and unreliable narrator

Minette Walters—similar use of psychological suspense

vehemently showing the effect it has on the lives of this community. In a sense, this novel shares some of the tragedy of noir. Cook's writing style is graceful, and he is a master at peeling away a layer at a time in agonizingly slow fashion for readers who will eagerly want to know what happened.

DISCUSSION QUESTIONS

In a noir novel, the characters are condemned to ruin from the beginning, without any hope of rescue. They know "how thin it is, and weaving, the tightrope we walk through life, how the smallest misstep can become a fatal plunge." What "missteps" in this story can you identify?

Is it wrong for Arthur Griswald to want Chatham School to be "studious, serious . . . disciplined," or does he love the school too much?

The motto of the school is *Veritas et Virtus* (truth and virtue). Does Arthur live up to that motto?

Was Jonathan Channing better to raise his daughter "as I saw fit . . . nor ever be bound by the false constraints of custom, ideology or blood"?

Is each of these statements true: "An artist should follow only his passions . . . all else is a noose around his neck" (p. 42); "Life is best lived at the edge of folly" (p. 50); "Art is like love. It's all or nothing." (p. 85)?

Who was the better father—Jonathan or Arthur?

Henry says Leland was like a father to him. When Arthur asks "what does that make me?" how do we answer?

Is Henry right when he says (p. 141) "we were not created in God's image at all, but in the image of Tantalus instead, the thing we most desire forever dancing before our eyes, and yet forever beyond our grasp"?

What fault is Elizabeth Channing's beauty? How do you react to Henry's statement (p. 82) that he has "a sense of woman as most lusty and desirable when poised at the edge of murder"?

Does Leland have good reasons for abandoning his family for Elizabeth?

Henry says "we have never discovered why, given the brevity of life and the depth of our need and the force of our passions, we do not pursue our own individual happiness with an annihilating zeal" (p. 221). Does any character do that in this novel?

How would you describe Abigail Reed's love for Leland? How tragic a figure is Abigail Reed?

Is Mildred Griswald correct to reject Henry's romantic vision of love and focus on the betrayal of Abigail Reed? Why does Mildred's revelation of Abigail's concerns end the love between her and Arthur?

"Be careful what you do for evil on itself doth back recoil," says Arthur Griswald, but Henry says "he could not have imagined how wrong he was." Do good deeds have the same fate as evil?

Do you agree that (p. 21) "it is the tragic fate of goodness to lack the vast attraction of romance"?

Why does Elizabeth offer no defense at her trial?

Does Henry act out of goodness? How guilty should Henry feel? What is the true meaning of the Leland's statement, "Sometimes I wish that she were dead"?

Can Mary offer absolution to Henry at the end of the novel?

See standard questions in the Introduction for more questions.

◇◇◆◇◇

Stephen Dobyns

The Church of Dead Girls

Stephen Dobyns was born in 1941 in Orange, New Jersey, and is the son of an Episcopal minister. He attended Shimer College and Wayne State University before earning an M.F.A. from the University of Iowa. He has taught English, has worked as a reporter, and has been a writer since 1971. Besides being a novelist, Dobyns is an award-winning poet. All of the books in his long-running mystery series about private detective Charlie Bradshaw have "Saratoga" in the title.

Web site:
none
Reader's guide:
none

Plot summary: A small town is always affected by a tragedy and when a murder occurs it can topple the sense of well-being. But when the murder of Janice McNeal, a woman of ill repute, is followed by the disappearance of three girls, it completely fractures this community. The citizens of Aurelia, New York, are quick to take on roles and make decisions, while the rights of individuals are trampled with impunity. While Janice's son is one suspect, the high school biology teacher who narrates this creepy tale does nothing to eliminate himself from the list.

Publication date: 1997
Number of pages: 388
Geographic setting: New York, Aurelia
Time period: 1990s
Series notes: This is a stand-alone novel.
Subject headings: Children at risk; Missing persons; Serial killers

Appeal points: This is as much a horror novel as it is a crime story. Think of it as Shirley Jackson's *The Lottery* on steroids. Dobyns does a wonderful job of mixing a literate style with the psychological thriller. Parts of this novel may be too intense for some readers.

Readalikes

Thomas H. Cook's *The Chatham School Affair*—similar sense of place

Reginald Hill's *On Beulah Height*—similar use of plot

Anthony Pyper's *Lost Girls*—similar use of plot

Minette Walters' *The Sculptress*—similar use of psychological suspense

DISCUSSION QUESTIONS

How comfortable were you with the narrator's voice?

Who is really telling us this story?

Is the point of view consistent?

Did the author evoke a sense of place?

Why are there no stable relationships in this town?

Does the crime cause the terror, or does it simply reveal what is hidden in this town?

Is Aaron's cause noble?

What is wrong with the IIR?

What is wrong with the Friends of Sharon Malloy?

A town can "turn to the best" (p. 335), but whom should we really trust?

See standard questions in the Introduction for more questions.

◇◇◆◇◇

Arthur Conan Doyle

The Hound of the Baskervilles

Arthur Conan Doyle was born in 1859 in Edinburgh, Scotland. Doyle earned a B.M. from Edinburgh University in 1881 and an M.D. in 1885. He worked as a physician until 1891 and served as a surgeon in the Boer War during 1900. Doyle was made famous by his Sherlock Holmes stories, but besides these detective yarns he wrote historical novels, speculative fiction, horror stories, domestic comedy, sports stories, poetry, and plays. His first short story appeared in 1879, and the author continued to write most of his life. His later years were spent investigating and defending spiritualism. He was twice married and had five children. In 1930 he died in Sussex, England.

Web site:
http://www.sirar
thurconandoyle.com
Reader's guide:
none

Plot summary: Legend has it that a hound-from-hell ripped out the throat of the evil Hugo Baskerville on the moors of Devonshire. Now years later, his family is still cursed with this legend. According to Dr. James Mortimer, heir-apparent Charles Baskerville is murdered by the rabid dog. Mortimer feels threatened enough to hire Sherlock Holmes to solve the mystery of the haunting hound and protect the next in line, Henry Baskerville. While Holmes disappears for a major portion of the book, Dr. John Watson is left to fend for himself and help their client. When the great detective finally reappears, it is to solve the threat of the ghostly animal.

Publication date: 1901

Number of pages: 249

Geographic setting: England, Devonshire, Dartmoor, Grimpen Mire

Time period: 1880s

Series notes: There are four novels and fifty-six short stories that make up the Holmes canon.

Subject headings: Dogs; Moors; Supernatural

Appeal points: "Mr. Holmes, they were the footprints of a gigantic hound!" The creepy nature of this gothic tale is fascinating to readers. It is especially interesting to read because this is the period after Doyle killed Holmes to get rid of him, only to be forced to bring him back because of popular demand. So, he craftily set the tale in 1899, prior to Holmes' death. Even so, Holmes spends a great deal of time hidden from the reader, which may or may not appeal to some. This novel will work with a novel-into-film discussion.

Similar titles: Wilkie Collins' *The Moonstone*—similar sense of place and style

DISCUSSION QUESTIONS

How did the author evoke the setting of the Grimpen Mire?

Does an element of the supernatural help or hurt a good mystery story?

What elements of this novel can you identify as either gothic, horror, or mystery?

While Holmes went missing, did you enjoy having Dr. Watson at center stage?

How big a buffoon is Dr. Watson?

What role did Barrymore serve in the novel?

Why did the author include Dr. Frankland?

How did the author make the sad story of Selden plausible?

See standard questions in the Introduction for more questions.

◇◇◆◇◇

Daphne du Maurier

Rebecca

Daphne du Maurier was born in 1907 in London, England, the daughter of actors. In 1932 she married Frederick Arthur Montague Browning, a lieutenant general. They had three children. Ms. du Maurier was a full-time writer from 1931 until her death in Cornwall in 1989. She published fifteen novels over her career, as well as short stories, nonfiction, and plays. In 1969 she received the Dame Commander, Order of the British Empire.

Web site:
http://www.dumaurier.org
Reader's guide:
none

Plot summary: "Last night I dreamt I went to Manderley again." This opening line begins the sad tale of the second Mrs. de Winter. When she falls for her husband Maxim, little does she know that she will be taken to his estate Manderley, where the ghost of the first Mrs. de Winter haunts the grounds while the hostile housekeeper Mrs. Danvers rules the manor. As the true story of the death of her rival is revealed, it tests the courage of the young bride.

Publication date: 1938
Number of pages: 357
Geographic setting: England, Cornwall

Time period: 1930s
Series notes: This is a stand-alone novel.
Subject headings: Estates; Marriage
Appeal points: This novel won a National Book Award in 1938. In 2000, the novel was given a special Anthony Award as the novel of the century. This dramatic tale of triumph over isolation should appeal to all readers. The mystery of what happened to Rebecca should sustain all mystery and suspense readers.

Readalikes

Jonathan Aycliffe's *A Garden Lost in Time*—similar use of family secrets

Emily Bronte's *Wuthering Heights*—similar sense of romance

Ruth Rendell's *The Crocodile Bird*—similar use of plot

DISCUSSION QUESTIONS

What attracts Maxim to Mrs. Van Hopper's companion?

Why does du Maurier label her novel *Rebecca* but never give a first name to the second Mrs. de Winter?

Why is Mrs. Danvers so fiercely loyal to Rebecca?

What role does Favell play in the story?

Why can Maxim not let go of the memory of Rebecca?

Does Maxim really love our narrator?

When the truth is revealed, why is the punishment to lose Manderley?

Why does Mrs. de Winter love Maxim?

See standard questions in the Introduction for more questions.

◇◇◆◇◇

David Ellis

Line of Vision

David Ellis graduated from Northwestern Law School and is an attorney in private practice in Chicago, where he lives with his wife Susan. He published this novel in 2001 and since has written *Life Sentence* (2003), *Jury of One* (2004), and *In the Company of Liars* (2005).

Web site:
http://www.davidellis.com
Reader's guide:
none

Plot summary: Investment banker Marty Kalish has been having an affair with a married woman named Rachel Reinhardt. When her husband Derrick disappears, Marty becomes suspect number one. Eventually, Marty is arrested and goes on trial. Marty is guilty of something, but exactly what is only explained as the novel unfolds. One thing is for certain: Marty's narrative is not to be trusted.

Number of pages: 407
Geographic setting: Illinois, Highland Woods
Time period: 2000s
Series notes: This is a stand-alone novel.
Subject headings: Adultery; Courtroom dramas; Trials
Appeal points: *Line of Vision* won the Edgar Allan Poe Award for Best First Novel by an American Author from the Mystery Writers of America. For

Readalikes

Minette Walters' *The Sculptress*—similar use of unreliable plot development

readers who like to be manipulated, this novel will be a stand out. It is one of the most frustrating books to read because of the nature of the narrator. Fans of courtroom thriller writers like Scott Turow and John Grisham should love this work.

DISCUSSION QUESTIONS

Did you like the author's technique of using short chapters?

On page 236, Marty provides a list of behaviors that he practices. What does this list tell us about Marty?

Is it fair to say Marty has an inability to commit?

Does Marty fear intimacy?

What is Marty's reason for his initial need to confess to the crime and save Rachel?

Do you like Marty?

Do you like Rachel?

Do you believe what you are told about Derrick?

Does our legal system work?

How far into the future does Marty see and how prepared is he for the eventual revelation of "the truth"?

How would you describe this book to a friend?

See standard questions in the Introduction for more questions.

◇◇◆◇◇

Jim Fergus

The Wild Girl: The Notebooks of Ned Giles, 1932

Jim Fergus lives in Arizona, where he works as a freelance journalist. He is the author of two nonfiction books: *A Hunter's Road* (1992) and *The Sporting Road* (1999). His first novel, *One Thousand White Women: The Journals of May Dodd*, published in 1998, was the winner of the Mountains and Plains Booksellers Award.

Web site:
http://www.readinggroup
guides.com/guides3/wild_girl1
.asp#aboutthisbook

Reader's guide:
none

Plot summary: Ned Giles is a teenage photographer who volunteers to join the Great Apache Expedition. The expedition is going into the Sierra Madre Mountains of Mexico to hunt for a kidnapped seven-year-old boy. Leaving from Douglas, Arizona, the expedition team is made up of an odd combination of adventurers, scientists, newspapermen, and even a gay college man. What begins as high adventure turns wicked under the leadership of Chief of Police Leslie Gatlin, especially after the capture of La Niña Bronca, the wild girl the expedition will try to use as trade bait for the boy. With the added perspective Ned receives from the two Native Americans who are the guides for the expedition, he begins to think that the real crime may not be the first kidnapping.

Publication date: 2005
Number of pages: 368
Geographic setting: Mexico, Sonora, Bauispe
Time period: 1930s
Series notes: This is a stand-alone novel.

Subject headings: Apaches; Coming of age; Photography; Romance; The West

Appeal points: This novel shifts the definition of crime novel in a radical direction. It could be used with groups who do not want to read a crime story, but will accept a historical novel. The issue of terrorism is brought to the forefront, as well as issues of ethnic cleansing. It also works as a coming of age novel and may have special appeal to male readers.

Readalikes

Margaret Atwood's *The Blind Assassin*—similar use of a plot within a plot

Harper Lee's *To Kill a Mockingbird*—similar coming-of-age story

DISCUSSION QUESTIONS

Ned's journals preserved his "progress, or lack thereof, as a photographer." Which would be more powerful to you, an actual copy of his photo of La Niña Bronca or his words about it?

Ned believes his story is truer because it is told as it happens, rather than recounted from memory by an old man. How much can we trust this seventeen-year-old narrator?

Big Ned says (p. 127) that "the camera never lies, only the person behind the camera." What does this mean to you?

Is "the photographer's only responsibility to tell the truth" (p. 38)?

How would you have reacted on this journey if you were Margaret?

What role does Tolley serve in the novel?

What does La Niña Bronca mean to Flowers when he captures her?

Is Indigo Juan a terrorist or a freedom fighter?

What separates a man like Flowers from a man like Indigo Juan?

Who do you understand better: Joseph or Albert?

Ned asks, "What good is a photograph if it cannot save a girl's life?" How would you answer that question?

Why do you agree or disagree with the choice that Ned makes at the end of his adventure?

Who commits the worst crime in this novel?

See standard questions in the Introduction for more questions.

◇◇◆◇◇

Elizabeth George

Born Susan Elizabeth George in Warren, Ohio, George moved with her family to California when she was a baby. She later earned a college degree and taught school, at one point receiving an award as Orange County teacher of the year. When she published her first novel, George quit the teaching profession. She was married for twenty-four years, but is currently divorced from her husband, who still is her business manager. George won the Anthony Award, the Agatha Award, and France's Le Grand Prix de Litterature Policiere for her novel *A Great Deliverance*, as well as nominations for the Edgar and the Macavity awards. She has also been awarded Germany's MIMI for her novel *Well-Schooled in Murder*. The author lives in Huntington Beach, California, but she spends a great deal of time in her flat in South Kensington, England. She has two nonseries novels in *The Evidence Exposed* (1999) and *I, Richard* (2002), and she is the author of a writing manual called *Write Away* (2004).

> **Web site:**
> http://www.elizabethgeorgeonline
> .com/index.htm

Series notes: The novels in the Thomas Lynley are *A Great Deliverance* (1988), *Payment in Blood* (1989), *Well-Schooled in Murder* (1990), *A Suitable Vengeance* (1991), *For the Sake of Elena* (1992), *Missing Joseph* (1993), *Playing for the Ashes* (1994), *In the Presence of the Enemy* (1996), *Deception on His Mind* (1997), *In Pursuit of the Proper Sinner* (1999), *A Traitor to Memory* (2001), *A Place of Hiding* (2003), and *With No One as Witness* (2005).

A Great Deliverance

> **Reader's guide:**
> none

Plot summary: In Keldale Abbey, obese teen Roberta Teys is accused of chopping her father's head off with an axe. She then falls into a catatonic state, but not before saying, "I did it. I'm not sorry." Sent to this insular community to work on the case are Scotland Yard Inspector Thomas Lynley and his sergeant, Barbara Havers. Mismatched, the pair is divided by their class and their misunderstanding of each other. As they learn to respect each other, they also learn the deeply held secrets of this ancient village.

Publication date: 1988
Number of pages: 305
Geographic setting: England, Yorkshire, Keldale Abbey
Time period: 1980s
Subject heading: Patricide
Appeal points: This novel was the winner of the Agatha and Anthony awards for best first novel as well as the Grand Prix de Litterature Policiere. It was

also nominated for both the Edgar and Macavity awards. This novel was made into a television film by the BBC and would work in a novel-into-film discussion. The main appeal of this novel is the developing relationship between the two stars of the series as seen in this first novel.

> **Readalikes**
>
> Minette Walters' *The Sculptress*—similar use of character

DISCUSSION QUESTIONS

Havers thinks Lynley is a "fop." What do you think of Havers?

Why does Lynley fail to understand Havers?

Havers is described as deliberately keeping herself unattractive. When we meet her, she is essentially on probation for being unable to work with anyone. What is her problem?

Why would the Eighth Earl of Asherton want to be a homicide cop?

How well does Lynley balance his affection for Deborah against his need to use Allcourt-St. James?

What does George do to draw you into Roberta's world?

What twisted William into the man he became?

Does Roberta make the right choice, or the only choice?

Is justice served?

See standard questions in the Introduction for more questions.

◇◇◆◇◇

A Traitor to Memory

　　Plot summary: In the eleventh novel to feature New Scotland Yard Detective Inspector Thomas Lynley, the story begins with the hit-and-run murder of Katie Waddington, a therapist who treats sexually dysfunctional clients. Then, Eugenie Davies suffers the same fate. Suspicion falls on her violin-virtuoso son, who is deep in therapy because his music has deserted him when he faces an audience. Or could it be that he has never gotten over the death of his sister for which Katja Wolfe went to jail. Other suspects for the hit-and-run are available for examination by Lynley and his partners, Detective Constable Barbara Havers and Winston Nkata. For the cops, the job is harder when one of their own may be compromised by the evidence in the case. But the key to unlocking who did the deed lies in the lost memories of the former child prodigy.

　　Publication date: 2001

<table>
<tr><td>

Readalikes

Reginald Hill's *On Beulah Height*—similar use of music as a theme

P. D. James' series about Adam Dagliesh—similar style of detection

Minette Walters—similar use of suspense

</td></tr>
</table>

Number of pages: 722

Geographic setting: England, London

Time period: 1990s

Subject headings: Hit-and-run accidents; Music; Violins

Appeal points: Several of George's novels have been filmed for television by the BBC and have been broadcast in the United States on PBS' *Mystery*. This long-running series has a continuing cast of characters that will hold interest for the readers even if this is the only book they read. Part of the interest in George's work is to see how an American can handle crafting mysteries set in Britain. While a lot of the novels in *Read 'Em Their Writes* are not true mysteries, George does try to stay within the confines of the "play fair" mystery with this novel.

DISCUSSION QUESTIONS

What image of Katie Waddington did you retain from the book?

In therapy, Gideon reveals that his problems may be linked to "abnormality leading to crisis." Thinking of each character, including the detectives, what abnormalities can you identify?

What should society do with people like Tongue Man?

Gideon declares (p. 524) that "people don't exist outside what they do." How do you define a person's existence?

What does the sheepdog that Gideon discovers while talking to his father (p. 217) mean to you?

Does Malcolm stand by Frances out of love or duty?

Lynley makes a decision to keep Webberly's letters a secret from everyone except Havers. Do you think his action was justified?

See standard questions in the Introduction for more questions.

◇◇◆◇◇

George Dawes Green

The Caveman's Valentine

George Dawes Green was born in 1954 in Idaho, the son of a newspaper man. He attended high school in Georgia. In the late 1970s and early 1980s, he wrote for the *Suburbia Today* magazine in New York City. From 1984 until 1991, he owned a clothing manufacturing and exporting business in Guatemala. He has been a full-time writer since 1991. He has also written the screenplay for this novel and the novel *The Juror* (1995). He lives in Key West, Florida.

Web site:
none
Reader's guide:
none

Plot summary: Romulus Ledbetter graduated from the Juilliard School of Music, but his quest to understand the music he loved led him to a life of mental illness. Now living in a cave in Manhattan's Inwood Park, he stumbles over the corpse of a photographer's model named Scotty Gales. He decides to find the killer who he believes works for the evil Cornelius Gould Stuyvesant, a man who rules the world from high atop the Chrysler Building.

Publication date: 1994

Number of pages: 323

Geographic setting: New York, New York (Inwood Park)

Time period: 1990s

Series notes: This is a stand-alone novel.

Subject headings: Homeless; Inwood Park, New York City; Paranoia

Appeal points: This novel was a New York Notable title and won the Edgar Award as the best first novel of the year. The lead character is so unique that one of the attractions of the story is watching the author as he tries to pull off the plot without losing control of his detective. The social issues raised in the novel will make for a lively discussion.

Readalikes

Mark Haddon's *The Curious Incident of the Dog in the Night-Time*—similar use of a challenged character

Laurie King's *To Play the Fool*—similar use of a challenged character

DISCUSSION QUESTIONS

Which aspect of this novel was more interesting to you: the mystery plot or the examination of the issue of mental health care in America?

How would you react if you walked past Ledbetter on the streets of your hometown?

How did the author convince you that Ledbetter is capable of finding a killer?

What is lacking in our society that a person like Ledbetter is living in a cave in a park?

In what ways does success in the arts play an evil role in this novel?

What purpose does Cornelius Gould Stuyvesant serve in the novel?

What should Lulu do about her father?

Why does Ledbetter choose not to go home?

See standard questions in the Introduction for more questions.

◇◇◄►◇◇

Graham Greene

The Third Man

Graham Greene was born in 1904 in Berkhamsted, Hertfordshire, England. He earned a B.A. from Balliol College, Oxford. Greene was a film critic in his early years. Besides this title, he wrote many novels, plays, and screenplays, earning himself a literary reputation. Greene was married to Vivien and they had two children. He died in 1991 in Vevey, Switzerland.

Plot summary: Harry Lime of the International Refugee Office has invited his friend Rollo Martins to Vienna. Normally a writer of pulp Westerns, Rollo's supposed assignment will be to write about the plight of international refugees. But when Rollo arrives in Vienna, he learns that Harry has been killed in a car accident. Anna Schmidt, Harry's lover, believes that the accident may have been murder. She could be right, considering that the police inform Rollo that Lime was a despicable criminal. A witness tells Rollo that a third man was at the accident scene, but then Rollo sees Harry on the streets of Vienna. When Rollo goes on a quest to discover the truth in the shattered city, he learns a horrible fact that forces him to administer justice for an unspeakable crime.

> **Web site:**
> none
> **Reader's guide:**
> none

Publication date: 1950
Number of pages: 157
Geographic setting: Austria, Vienna
Time period: 1950s
Series notes: This is a stand-alone novel.
Subject headings: Refugees; World War II
Appeal points: It is almost impossible to separate the filmed version of this story from this novella because the work was basically written as an outline for the film's script. While Rollo is the hero in this tale, his friend Harry Lime is a fascinating character whose true nature is not revealed until the final pages of the book. The postwar period and the city of Vienna should appeal to all historical fiction readers.

> **Readalikes**
> John LeCarre's *The Spy Who Came in from the Cold*—similar use of theme in a thriller

DISCUSSION QUESTIONS

How did the author recreate the horror of a city destroyed by conflict?

Do the consequences of World War II create a man like Harry, or does he just take advantage of the conflict?

How do you explain a man like Harry Lime?

Which of his characteristics could be considered childlike?

Is Harry amoral, diseased, or more normal than we would like to think?

Why does Anna become dependent on Harry? Why do you believe she may be in love with Harry?

How would you answer the question, "If I said you can have twenty thousand pounds for every dot that stops, would you really, old man, tell me to keep the money"?

Does Rollo make the right decisions at the end of the novel? Why could his decisions be considered a betrayal?

See standard questions in the Introduction for more questions.

◇◇◆◇◇

David Guterson

Snow Falling on Cedars

David Guterson was born in 1956 in Seattle, Washington, the third of five children. His father was a criminal defense attorney. Guterson earned a B.A. in English from the University of Washington in 1978. In 1982 he earned an M.A. in creative writing from the same university. He was a high school English teacher on Bainbridge Island, Washington, from 1984 until 1994. While teaching, he wrote magazine articles, including some published in *Sports Illustrated* and *Harper's* magazine. He is now a contributing editor at *Harper's*. His first book, a collection of short stories called *The Country Ahead of Us, the Country Behind*, was published in 1989. He has also written *East of the Mountains* (1999). In 1992 a nonfiction title called *Why Homeschooling Makes Sense* was published. He is married, and he and his wife Robin have four children.

Plot summary: On the Puget Sound island of San Piedro, a community struggles with the lingering effects of World War II. Despite having sent its sons to fight in Europe, the Japanese community is ostracized; and the community is divided physically as well as racially. When conflict develops over ownership of land between a white man and his Japanese neighbors, it leads to a charge of murder. As the trial develops, the author shifts time to slowly reveal the dark history of this community and to reveal who carries the guilt for the sad events as they unfold.

> **Web site:**
> none
>
> **Readers guide:**
> http://www.randomhouse
> .com/vintage/read/snow

Publication date: 1994

Number of pages: 354

Geographic setting: Washington (State), Puget Sound, San Piedro Island

Time period: 1950s

Series notes: This is a stand-alone novel.

Subject headings: Courtroom dramas; Japanese Americans; Journalists; Romance; Trials; Winter weather

Appeal points: Guterson's novel won the PEN/Faulkner Award for Fiction, the American Booksellers Book of the Year Award, the Folger Shakespeare Library, the Barnes & Noble Discovery Award, and the Pacific Northwest Booksellers Award. It was made into a film by Universal Pictures in 1999 and makes an excellent novel-into-film discussion title. This novel appeals to readers who want a rich, literary read. Its efforts to explain race relations make it useful in classrooms as well as book discussions.

> **Readalikes**
>
> Thomas H. Cook's *The Chatham School Affair*—similar style of plot
>
> Harper Lee's *To Kill a Mockingbird*—similar style of plot
>
> Cormac McCarthy's *All the Pretty Horses*—similar coming-of-age novel

DISCUSSION QUESTIONS

What did you enjoy about the author's writing style?

What did you think of the way the author uses time in this novel?

How did this novel work as a mystery? Were there enough clues to solve the crime?

How did this novel work as a legal thriller? Did you enjoy the courtroom drama?

The title refers to the snow that falls on the island. What role does the weather play in this story?

The island of San Piedro appears as divided as the people who live there. Can you identify which areas "belong" to which people?

What makes the island's residents racist, and what does not?

In interviews, the author worried about getting the Japanese American characters right? How did he succeed or fail?

How evil is Etta Heine?

How much of this novel's consequences can be blamed on the lingering effects of World War II?

How do you judge the forces of the law and their decision to arrest Kabuo and assume Carl's death was a homicide?

What would make you call Carl a "good man"?

If Ishmael and Hatsue had married, how would you describe their future?

What are the similarities between Kabuo and Carl?

What are the similarities between Kabuo and Ishmael?

What has really caused Ishmael's cold-blooded detachment to life?

Has Ishmael wasted his life?

Is the strawberry farm worth all this tragedy?

What does the last sentence of the book mean?

See standard questions in the Introduction for more questions.

◇◇◆◇◇

Barbara Hambly

A Free Man of Color

Barbara Hambly was born in San Diego, California, in 1951. In 1975, she earned an M.A. in medieval history from the University of California—Riverside. She held a variety of jobs related to writing, and her first novel was published in 1982. She has gone on to write fantasy, romance, vampire, Star Trek, historical, and historical mystery novels. Hambly has been the President of the Science Fiction Writers of America (1994–1996), a Locus Award winner, and a multiple Nebula Award nominee. The author lives in Los Angeles.

Plot summary: Benjamin January is an internationally trained doctor and a free Creole, but in the New Orleans of 1833 he is not allowed to practice medicine because he is of mixed blood. While working as piano player at a Carnival revelry, he becomes involved in the search for Madeleine Trepagier's family jewels when this white woman attends the octoroon, or the ball for the people of color. The jewels are in the possession of Angelique Crozat, mistress to Madeleine's dead husband. When Angelique is murdered, January takes up the cause of finding the murderer. Allying himself with a sympathetic policeman named Abishag Shaw, January tries to retain his dignity and solve the crime.

> **Web site:**
> http://www.barbarahambly.com
> **Reader's guide:**
> none

Publication date: 1997
Number of pages: 311
Geographic setting: Louisiana, New Orleans
Time period: 1830s
Series notes: *A Free Man of Color* is the first book in the Benjamin January series. The other titles are *Fever Season* (1998), *Graveyard Dust* (1999), *Sold Down the River* (2000), *Die upon a Kiss* (2001), *Wet Grave* (2002), and *Days of the Dead* (2003).
Subject headings: African Americans; Mardi Gras
Appeal points: The novel's sense of heroism makes the lead character a very sympathetic protagonist. The author's ability to recreate this unique setting among the many historical novels being published also appeals. If the reader enjoys this book, there are many others in the series to enjoy as well.

> **Readalikes**
> Walter Mosley's Easy Rawlins series—similar use of character
> Anne Perry—similar historical fiction writer

DISCUSSION QUESTIONS

Does this book work as a historical novel?

What did you learn about New Orleans that was new?

Can you name another society that is equally stratified as 1830s New Orleans?

How would you picture New Orleans society if Louisiana had not been sold to the United States?

What elements of the Black Code can you name?

What makes a good mystery protagonist to you?

Does Benjamin January share those characteristics?

What are the elements that make up Benjamin January?

What is the role of women in this society?

Is this an epic or a melodrama?

How did you react to the vast panorama of characters presented?

Who was your favorite character besides January?

Did you like the writing style?

How did the mystery work for you?

See standard questions in the Introduction for more questions.

◇◇◆◇◇

Dashiell Hammett

The Maltese Falcon

Samuel Dashiell Hammett was born in 1894 in St. Mary, Maryland. He attended Baltimore Polytechnic Institute but left high school at age fourteen. Hammett held a variety of jobs but worked for the Pinkerton National Detective Agency from 1915 until 1918 and again from 1919 until 1921. Hammett served in the U.S. Army Ambulance Corps from 1918 through 1919. For the rest of his life he suffered from the tuberculosis he contracted while serving, and from alcoholism. In 1921, Hammett married Josephine Dolan, a nurse he met in a hospital. The couple had a contentious relationship that led to a separation in 1927 and a formal divorce in 1937. They had two daughters. Hammett worked for the Albert S. Samuels Jewelers of San Francisco as an advertising copywriter from 1922 until 1927. In 1922 his first story was published in *The Smart Set*. His first detective fiction appeared in *Black Mask* magazine in 1923. His short stories featured a nameless detective branded The Continental Op. Besides this novel about Sam Spade, his books include *Red Harvest* (1927—The Continental Op), *The Dain Curse* (1929—The Continental Op), *The Glass Key* (1931—hood Ned Beaumont), *The Thin Man* (1934—Nick and Nora Charles), and various short-story collections. In the 1930s, besides his own publications, Hammett worked as a screenwriter for a number of motion picture studios. Tragically, *The Thin Man* marked the end of Hammett's writing career. Hammett again served his country as a sergeant in the U.S. Army Signal Corps from 1942 until 1945. Throughout the 1920s and 1930s Hammett was active in Marxist organizations, which earned him a hearing in front of Congress and a jail term in 1951 for contempt. His later years were spent in the company of playwright Lillian Hellman and in dodging the Internal Revenue Service, which eventually garnisheed his royalties. He died in 1961 of lung cancer.

Plot summary: When the beautiful and captivating Miss Wonderly wanders into the Spade and Archer Detective Agency, Miles Archer agrees to follow her down a blind alley and ends up murdered. Sam Spade, Archer's partner, decides to avenge his death, and is given the opportunity when Miss Wonderly returns to the

Web site:
none
Reader's guide:
http://www.randomhouse.com/catalog/display.pperl?isbn=9780679722649&view=rg

agency, this time confessing to be Brigid O'Shaughnessy. Brigid blames a man named Floyd Thursby for Archer's death, and as Spade begins to investigate he discovers the real reason for the murder may be a jeweled bird known as the Maltese Falcon.

Publication date: 1930
Number of pages: 186
Geographic setting: California, San Francisco

Time period: 1920s

Series notes: Besides this novel, there is one collection of short stories featuring this detective called *The Adventures of Sam Spade* (1944—also: *A Man Called Spade*).

Subject heading: Antiquities

Readalikes
Raymond Chandler's Philip Marlowe series—similar style of private eye novel
Bill Pronzini's Nameless Detective series—similar style of private eye novel

Appeal points: This novel works in any novel-into-film discussion. The careful way that Hammett never allows the reader to know Sam Spade's true motivations makes him a fascinating character to dissect. This novel is the standard bearer for all private eye fiction, and most hard-boiled writing, so it is appealing to read one of the founding fathers of this genre.

DISCUSSION QUESTIONS

Raymond Chandler said of Hammett's writing, "Hammett took murder out of the Venetian vase and dropped it into the alley. . . . [He] gave murder back to the kind of people that commit it for reasons, not just to provide a corpse; and with the means at hand, not with hand-wrought dueling pistols, curare, and tropical fish." What things in this novel can you identify as different in his writing than from Hammett's contemporary, Agatha Christie?

How would you explain the character of Gutman?

In its time, *The Maltese Falcon* shocked readers because of the homosexual relationship in the novel. How did this affect you in trying to understand the behavior of Gutman and Wilmer?

What did the physical description of Sam Spade mean to you when the author states, "He looked rather pleasantly like a blond Satan"?

Is Sam Spade a romantic?

Why does Miles' widow believe Sam is capable of killing her husband?

How does Sam treat each of the three female characters in this book and how do they treat Sam? Do any of these relationships have a future?

How much is Spade aware of the deception when early in the book he says to Brigid, "You won't need much of anybody's help. You're good. You're very good. It's chiefly your eyes, I think, and that throb you get into your voice when you say things like 'Be generous, Mr. Spade'"?

Sam Spade lives by a code of behavior that has come to define the private eye as a fictional character. What elements of that code can you identify, and how did each affect the story?

How do you react to the hero of this novel saying, "I'm going to send you over. The chances are you'll get off with life. That means you'll be out again in twenty years. You're an angel. I'll wait for you. . . . If they hang you I'll always remember you"?

How do you react to the hero of this novel saying, "Don't be too sure I'm as crooked as I'm supposed to be"? Is Spade a good man doing bad things, or a bad man who decides to do one good thing?

Is Sam motivated by his personal loyalty to his partner, his professional integrity to carry out the wishes of his client, or is he a greedy little man who just missed getting a sweet deal?

Where is the Maltese Falcon?

See standard questions in the Introduction for more questions.

◇◇◆◇◇

Carolyn G. Hart

Letter from Home

Carolyn G. (William) Hart was born in 1936 in Oklahoma City, Oklahoma. She married Philip, an attorney, in 1958 and they had two children. Also in 1958, Hart earned a B.A. from the University of Oklahoma, Norman. After graduation, Hart worked as a reporter for the *Norman Transcript* in Norman. She began her career as a freelance writer in 1961. For three years in the 1980s, she was an assistant professor at the University of Oklahoma's School of Journalism and Mass Communications. Her first novel was published in 1975, and her first mystery novel, *Death on Demand,* was published in 1987. Altogether there are sixteen novels in the Death on Demand series. Also, she has written six novels about her journalist character Henrie O. Hart's novels have won the Agatha and Anthony awards for *Something Wicked*, the Agatha for *Dead Man's Island*, the Anthony for *Honeymoon with Murder*, the Macavity Award for *A Little Class on Murder*, and the Macavity Award and Agatha Award nominations for *Scandal in Fair Haven*. She lives in Oklahoma City.

Web site:
http://www.carolynhart.com
Reader's guide:
none

Plot summary: In an unnamed small town in Oklahoma in 1944, the local newspaper, desperate for help, hires thirteen-year-old Gretchen Gilman as a stringer. Faye Tatum, scorned for dancing in the bars while her husband, Clyde, is off to war, is strangled shortly after he returns on leave. The young Gilman writes a pivotal and sympathetic portrait of the dead woman that launches her into a career in journalism. Years later, Gilman receives a letter that directs her back to this rural setting where the real reason why Faye was murdered is revealed.

Publication date: 2003
Number of pages: 262
Geographic setting: Oklahoma

Time period: 1940s
Series notes: This is a stand-alone novel.
Subject headings: Journalists; Rural towns; World War II

Appeal points: This novel was nominated for the Pulitzer Prize for Fiction and won the Agatha Award for Best Mystery Novel of 2003. Its strength is that it is a female coming-of-age novel. Hart also manages to capture the character of the region, the time in history, and the people who populate this small town.

Readalikes

David Guterson's *Snow Falling on Cedars*—similar style of character in a coming-of-age novel

Elizabeth Inness-Brown's *Burning Marguerite*—similar use of plot

Harper Lee's *To Kill a Mockingbird*—similar use of theme

DISCUSSION QUESTIONS

What has made the difference between Barb and G. G.?

Is it proper that the Gazette hired a girl "almost" fourteen as a reporter?

How responsible is the media to report just "the facts" in a murder case?

Both Barb and Clyde are reluctant to be honest with the authorities. If they had, would this story have turned out better?

How should Lorraine have handled her return to her hometown with Sam?

Why does everyone hate Faye so fiercely?

How is religion portrayed in this novel?

What sense of World War II–era America do you get from this novel?

Does anyone have the right to lie, even for self-preservation?

What lessons did G. G. learn from her childhood experiences?

See standard questions in the Introduction for more questions.

◇◇◀▬◇◇

Carl Hiaasen

Tourist Season

Carl Hiaasen was born in 1953 in Fort Lauderdale, Florida, the son of a lawyer and a homemaker. He earned a B.S. from the University of Florida in 1974. Since then, Hiaasen has worked as a reporter or columnist. He has been married twice and has two children.

Plot summary: Brian Keyes is a former newspaper reporter who operates a private eye agency in Miami. A Shriner goes missing, possibly eaten by an alligator. The President of the local Chamber of Commerce has been chopped up, stuffed in a suitcase with an alligator shoved down his throat, and set to float in the bay. A terrorist group called Las Noches de Diciembre begins to make claims, and then a Canadian goes missing. When an old journalist pal seems a little too obsessed with the development of his beloved Florida and the influx of tourists, Keyes begins to wonder about the real motive behind the murders.

> **Web site:**
> http://www.carlhiaasen.com
> **Reader's guide:**
> none

Publication date: 1986
Number of pages: 272

> **Readalikes**
>
> Tim Dorsey's Serge Storm series—similar setting and style of character
>
> James W. Hall—similar setting and style of character
>
> Elmore Leonard—similar use of plot

Geographic setting: Florida, Miami
Time period: 1980s
Series notes: This is a stand-alone novel.
Subject heading: Tourism
Appeal points: Can a crime novel have a message and be funny at the same time? If the humor appeals to the reader, this novel will be a success. Some readers may find the humor a little too dark to laugh.

DISCUSSION QUESTIONS

How did the author use humor to deliver his message?

How did the author use dialog to develop his story?

Are there particular scenes or passages that you remember from this comic novel?

Is this novel ironic or absurd, or both?

How good a detective is Brian Keyes?

Hiaasen has claimed he wrote this book to drive tourists out of Florida. How did it make you feel?

Hiaasen's serious theme is the overdevelopment of Florida. How can we be more responsible when so many people want to live there?

See standard questions in the Introduction for more questions.

◇◇◆◇◇

Reginald Hill

On Beulah Height

Reginald Charles Hill was born in 1936 in West Hartlepool, Couny Durham, England. When he was a young boy, his family moved to County Cumberland. After grammar school, he served two years in military service, and then received a B.A. with honors in English from St. Catherine's College at Oxford. In 1960 he married Patricia Ruell. Hill worked as a secondary school teacher in Essex from 1962 until 1967. He then became a lecturer in English literature at the Doncaster College of Education in Yorkshire. His first novel, *A Clubbable Woman*, was published in 1970. By 1981, Hill was a full-time writer. He has written over fifty novels under his own name and the pseudonyms of Dick Morland, Patrick Ruell, and Charles Underhill. Hill has received an Edgar Award nomination for *The Spy's Wife*; the Crime Writers' Association Gold Dagger Award for *Bones and Silence*; and the Cartier Diamond Dagger for a lifetime contribution to crime writing in 1995. He lives in Ravenglass, Cumbria.

Web site:
http://www.randomhouse.com/
features/reghill
Reader's guide:
none

Plot summary: Fifteen years ago, the small village of Dendale in Yorkshire was flooded to create a reservoir. At the same time, the mysterious and fantastical legend Benny Lightfoot was blamed for the disappearance of three young girls, a crime never solved because Benny disappeared as well. Andy Dalziel was a cop on that case. Now, fifteen years later as Detective Superintendent, he is on the scene when a drought begins to expose the landscape and the locals are once again blaming Benny for the disappearance of seven-year-old Lorraine Dacre. Dalziel's partner, Chief Inspector Peter Pascoe, aids on the case while dealing with the illness of his young daughter. The culmination of the case whirls around a musical performance created by Dendale's celebrity mezzo-soprano Elizabeth Wulfstan that rekindles all the bitter memories of the missing children.

Publication date: 1998
Number of pages: 374
Geographic setting: England, Yorkshire, Dendale
Time period: 1980s, 1990s
Series notes: *A Clubbable Woman* (1970), *An Advancement of Learning* (1971), *Ruling Passion* (1973), *An April Shroud* (1975), *A Pinch of Snuff* (1978), *Pascoe's Ghost* (1979), *A Killing Kindness* (1980), *Deadheads* (1983), *Exit Lines* (1984), *Child's Play* (1987), *Under World* (1988), *Bones and Silence* (1990), *One Small Step* (1990), *Recalled to Life* (1992), *Pictures of Perfection* (1994), *The Wood Beyond* (1996), *Asking for the Moon* (1996), *On Beulah Height* (1998), *Arms and the Women* (1999), *Dialogues of the Dead* (2001), *Death's Jest-Book* (2003), and *Good Morning, Midnight* (2004).

Subject headings: Children at risk; Droughts; Reservoirs; Serial killers

Appeal points: Hill's novel is a great literary achievement in its ability to combine a ghost story with a contemporary murder mystery. He incorporates mythology with music as well as historical events with contemporary scenes. Because of those qualities, this novel may be a challenge to the traditional mystery reader. Dalziel and Pascoe's stories have been made into television productions, so this novel also works with novel-into-film discussions.

> **Readalikes**
>
> Margaret Atwood's *The Blind Assassin*—similar literary style
>
> J. Wallis Martin's *A Likeness in Stone*—similar use of plot
>
> Peter Robinson's *In a Dry Season*—similar use of plot

DISCUSSION QUESTIONS

What sense of place does this book have?

How do you feel about the people of Dendale being forced to move to a new community?

What reason can you think of both for and against staging the musical performance?

Andy Dalziel—is he God or Satan?

How would you describe Hill's technique in creating this novel?

Would you consider these books British Police Procedurals?

Why is it that important to be loved?

Who has illusions about love?

Who is truly loved?

See standard questions in the Introduction for more questions.

◇◇◆◇◇

Tony Hillerman

Dance Hall of the Dead

Anthony Hillerman was born in 1925 in Sacred Heart, Oklahoma, on his father's farm. He attended St. Mary's Academy, a boarding school for Pottawatomie Indian girls. Prior to World War II, he attended Oklahoma Agricultural & Mechanical College, but left for military service before graduating. Hillerman is a thrice decorated military veteran of World War II, having landed at Normandy and been wounded at Alsace. In 1948 he earned a B.A. from the University of Oklahoma. That same year, he married his wife Marie; they have six children, five of whom are adopted. Hillerman worked as a newspaper reporter and editor from 1948 until 1963. Since 1965 he has served in a variety of academic positions. In 1966 he earned an M.A. from the University of New Mexico. Having had numerous contacts with Native Americans throughout his life, Hillerman decided to create a mystery series featuring a Native American detective. The series was modeled on the Australian novels of Arthur Upfield that featured Napoleon Bonaparte, an Aborigine detective. His nonseries fiction includes *The Fly on the Wall* (1970) and *Finding Moon* (1995) while his nonfiction writing includes *Seldom Disappointed: A Memoir* (2001). Past President of the Mystery Writers of America, Hillerman was made a Grand Master by that organization in 1991.

Web site:
http://www.tonyhillermanbooks.com
Reader's guide:
none

Plot summary: Lieutenant Joe Leaphorn of the Navajo Tribal Police is investigating the disappearance of a young Navajo named George Bowlegs in cooperation with the Zuni Reservation police. When it is discovered that a young Zuni boy named Ernesto Cata, training for a Zuni ceremony, has been murdered, there are indications that the two cases are linked. Then George is found murdered as well. Covering the huge expanse of the tribal grounds, Leaphorn tries to follow the clues in the native sphere, but finds himself drawn toward the white culture for the reasons behind these murders.

Publication date: 1974

Number of pages: 166

Geographic setting: New Mexico, Four Corners; New Mexico, Navajo Reservation; New Mexico, Shiprock; New Mexico, Zuni Reservation

Time period: 1970s

Series notes: Setting his novels on the Navajo reservation that covers the four corners region of the United States, Hillerman first introduced Joe Leaphorn in *The Blessing Way* (1970), which was nominated for the Edgar Award as best first novel of the year. Besides *Dance Hall of the Dead*, the other Leaphorn novel is *Listening Woman* (1978). *People of Darkness* (1980) introduced a second Navajo character named Jim Chee, followed by *The Dark Wind* (1982) and *The Ghostway* (1984). The two characters meet in *Skinwalkers* (1986—an Anthony

Award winner) and share the following novels together: *A Thief of Time* (1988—a Macavity Award winner), *Talking God* (1989), *Coyote Waits* (1990), *Sacred Clowns* (1993), *The Fallen Man* (1996), *The First Eagle* (1998), *Hunting Badger* (1999), *The Wailing Wind* (2002), *The Sinister Pig* (2003), and *Skeleton Man* (2004).

Subject headings: Navajo; Zuni

Appeal points: This novel won the Edgar Award as the best mystery of the year. As an introduction to the Native American culture, all of Hillerman's novels try to open doors of respect and understanding for this way of life. The geographic setting should also appeal to readers interested in reading about nonurban settings.

Readalikes

Peter Bowen's Gabriel Du Pre series—similar use of setting

Margaret Coel's Vicky Cohen series—similar use of setting and character

James Doss' Charlie Moon series—similar use of setting and character

Jean Hager's Molly Bearclaw series—similar use of setting and character

Arthur Upfield's Napoleon Bonaparte series—similar use of character

---

DISCUSSION QUESTIONS

How is Joe Leaphorn different from your perspective of what a Native American is?

Why does Joe resent the initial assignment?

How many jurisdictions are crossed in this novel and what does each bring to the story?

How deep is Joe's faith in his ancestors' beliefs? In what world does he walk?

Is Joe a good cop?

Who should study the cultures of the Southwest? How much is enough, and when does it cross over into cultural destruction?

Do movements like Jason's Fleece usurp a culture, or are they healthy blends of two societies?

Should the stories of Native Americans be told by a non-Native author?

See standard questions in the Introduction for more questions.

◇◇◆◇◇

William Hoffman

Tidewater Blood

William Hoffman was born in 1925 in Charleston, West Virginia, the son of a coal miner. His parents divorced shortly after his birth. He was raised by his grand-mother and schooled at the Kentucky Military Institute. From 1943 until 1946, Hoffman served in the U.S. Army, where he saw action in Normandy and the Battle of the Bulge. He earned a B.A. from Hampden-Sydney College in 1949, and then did graduate studies at Washington and Lee University in law and at the University of Iowa Writers' Workshop. From 1952 until 1959, he was an assistant professor at Hampden-Sydney. At this point in his life he became a full-time writer. From 1966 until 1970, he was a writer-in-residence at the college. His first novel was published in 1957, and since then he has written over fifteen novels or collections of short stories. Hoffman married Alice Sue Richardson in 1957 and they have two daughters. He lives on a farm in Charlotte County, Virginia.

Plot summary: Vietnam vet and ex-con Charles Le Blanc is the black sheep of his blue-blood Virginia family, living on his own in his shack in the woods. When a bomb kills Charles' older brother, wife, and children while they were celebrating the 250th anniversary of his family at their ancestral home, Bellerive, Charles becomes suspect number one. When the evidence is not strong enough to hold him, his first choice is to flee to Montana. But when he discovers someone has pursued him, Charles decides to find out who killed his family.

Web site:
none
Reader's guide:
none

Publication date: 1998
Number of pages: 290
Geographic setting: Montana; Virginia, Tidewater; West Virginia
Time period: 1990s
Series notes: This is a stand-alone novel.

Subject heading: Family feuds

Appeal points: *Tidewater Blood* received the North American Branch of the International Association of Crime Writers' Hammett Award in 1998. This novel is a gritty look at a family feud gone wrong. The goal of Charles to avenge his family's murder should redeem him as a character in the mold of the antihero.

Readalikes

Lee Child's Jack Reacher series—similar use of suspense and character

DISCUSSION QUESTIONS

What words would you use to describe this book to a friend?

What "sense of place" images can you remember from the book?

All Charlie talks about is getting away—why does he choose to live very near Bellerive?

Every time Charlie introduces himself to a stranger, he uses a different name. Why?

How bad a man was Charlie's father?

Why could you like Charlie?

What are the reasons for Charlie's antisocial behavior?

Why do civilized people judge Charlie—yet odd strangers take him in without questions?

Why do the police hate Charlie so much?

Could you be as persistent as Charlie if you had to survive?

What is the book's theme?

See standard questions in the Introduction for more questions.

◇◇◆◇◇

Elizabeth Inness-Brown

Burning Marguerite

Elizabeth Inness-Brown was born in 1954 in Rochester, New York, the daughter of a surgeon. In 1976, she earned a B.A. in English from St. Lawrence University. Her M.F.A. in creative writing, earned in 1978, is from Columbia University. Inness-Brown has held a number of positions in various academic settings, and is now on the faculty of Vermont College. She published two collections of short stories before publishing this novel. She lives in Colchester, Vermont.

Plot summary: On Grain Island, James Jack lives an idyllic life until one winter he discovers the dead body of his "aunt" Tante, the woman who raised him after his parents' death when he was age four. As it turns out, this will not be the only crime or death that will have to be explained. This novel's parallel narrative is split between Jack's third-person isolation and the first-person voice of Tante. Jack's path to the truth will lead him to a troubled woman named Faith, who might be his future. Tante's mysteries, including her time in New Orleans, will keep the reader guessing about the realities sheltered on this tiny island.

Publication date: 2002
Number of pages: 237
Geographic setting: Louisiana, New Orleans; New England, Grain Island
Time period: 1990s

Series notes: This is a stand-alone novel.
Subject headings: Coming of age; Islands; Romance

Appeal points: This novel is emotionally engaging, as the characters' complex psychological reasons for their conduct are played out over a setting that is unique and purposeful. The love story should appeal to some readers. In a sense, the agonizingly slow revelation of the truth has some connection to the horror genre.

Web site:
none

Reader's guide:
http://www.randomhouse.com/catalog/
display.pperl?isbn=9780375726224
&view=rg

Readalikes

David Guterson's *Snow Falling on Cedars*—similar use of coming-of-age plot

Harper Lee's *To Kill a Mockingbird*—similar use of coming-of-age plot

---

DISCUSSION QUESTIONS

Does this novel have a distinctive sense of place?

Could this have been set in a location other than this particular island?

What role does nature play in this novel?

Is Tante a woman of her times or a woman unique in her behaviors and attitudes?

Did the island make Tante or did she create her own challenges?

Tante's leaving the island heaps blame on her for her ill treatment of her parents—yet it is her sacrifice that allows them to be influential on the island. Is this irony or tragedy?

Tante says (p. 29), "that one could love only oneself, and that not very much." Is this true?

Inness-Brown said in an interview, "each of my characters should find some happiness in love." Do they?

How does fire serve to advance the story and the theme?

Who is the moth in the parable told on page 183?

Does Tante make the right decision for herself in fleeing after Daniel's murder (p. 213)?

On page 178, Tante says her tragedy meant "genuine proof that virtue was forever beyond my grasp." Is she right?

Can you identify some of the author's techniques in telling this story?

See standard questions in the Introduction for more questions.

◇◇◆◇◇

P. D. James

An Unsuitable Job for a Woman

Phyllis Dorothy James was born in 1920 in Oxford, England. Prior to World War II, she worked as an assistant stage manager in a Cambridge theater. She married Ernest Conner Bantry White, a doctor, in 1941 and they had two daughters. Because Ernest was traumatized by the war and could not work, James was forced to work full time to support her family. Her husband died in 1964. From 1949 until 1968, James was the principal administrative assistant for a hospital board. She then did the same work for the Department of Home Affairs of the Police Department from 1968 until 1972. She subsequently moved to the Criminal Policy Department, where she stayed until 1979. She has been a full-time writer since then. James received the Silver Dagger and Edgar awards for *Shroud for a Nightingale* and the Silver Dagger Award for *The Black Tower*. She was awarded the Diamond Dagger for lifetime achievement from the Crime Writers' Association. In addition to her crime novels, James has written an autobiography, *Time to Be in Earnest: A Fragment of an Autobiography* (1999). In 1983 she was awarded the Order of the British Empire (OBE); in 1991 she was made a life peer of the United Kingdom with the title Baroness James of Holland Park.

> **Web site:**
> http://www.randomhouse.com/
> features/pdjames
> **Reader's guide:**
> none

Plot summary: After her partner and mentor Bernie Pryde commits suicide, Cordelia Gray finds herself owner of a detective agency. Determined to carry on and be successful, she accepts a case offered by Sir Ronald Callender. He wants to discover why his son committed suicide so shortly after leaving Cambridge. Cordelia travels to Duxford to interview the couple that hosted Mark Callender, and discovers that a Sergeant Maskell has also been asking questions about Mark's death.

Publication date: 1972
Number of pages: 216
Geographic setting: England, Cambridge
Time period: 1970s
Series notes: There is one more novel about Cordelia Gray called *The Skull beneath the Skin* (1982).

Subject headings: Academia; Female detectives

Appeal points: This novel was a nominee for the Edgar Award. It is a precursor to the wave of female private detectives that have swept themselves onto the bestseller lists. Cordelia is a very vulnerable character and therefore should win sympathy with most readers.

> **Readalikes**
>
> Liza Cody's Anna Lee series—similar style of private eye novel
>
> Michelle Spring's Laura Principal series—similar style of private eye novel

DISCUSSION QUESTIONS

What from her convent education can Cordelia apply to the job of detective?

Why does Bernie leave the agency to Cordelia? What does he see in her that she does not see in herself?

How is Cordelia's dogged interest in Mark's death tied to her feelings of abandonment by Bernie?

What keeps Cordelia from blending in with Mark's friends?

How does Cordelia lose herself in Mark's story?

Knowing how she feels, why does Cordelia put Mark's relatives through the same emotional experience she has been through?

Is Cordelia a suitable woman for the job?

See standard questions in the Introduction for more questions.

◇◇◆◇◇

Laurie King

To Play the Fool

Laurie Richardson was born in 1952 in Oakland, California, the daughter of a furniture restorer and a librarian. She married Noel Q. King in 1977. They have two children. King earned a B.A. from the University of California, Santa Cruz, in 1977 and an M.A. from Graduate Theological Union in 1984. Besides her Kate Martinelli series, King writes about Mary Russell, Sherlock Holmes' partner, in *The Beekeeper's Apprentice; or, On the Segregation of the Queen* (1994—Agatha Award nomination), *A Monstrous Regiment of Women* (1995—Nero Wolfe Award), *A Letter of Mary* (1997), *The Moor* (1998), *O Jerusalem* (1999), *Justice Hall* (2002), *The Game* (2004), and *Locked Rooms* (2005). King's stand-alone novels include *A Darker Place* (1999), *Folly* (2001—Macavity Award winner), and *Keeping Watch*, (2003—Barry Award nominee). She has also written a science fiction novel *Califia's Daughters* (2004) under the pseudonym Leigh Richards. She lives in Freedom, California.

Plot summary: Kate Martinelli's new case dealing with the murder of a homeless man in Golden Gate Park brings a special challenge to the detective. First a dog is given a Viking funeral, then a few weeks later, so is his owner. Her chief suspect is Brother Erasmus who only speaks in literary quotations from Shakespeare and the Bible. Is he a Holy Fool, or is he a murderer?

Web site:
http://www.laurierking.com

Reader's guide:
none

Publication date: 1995
Number of pages: 260
Geographic setting: California, Berkeley; California, San Francisco
Time period: 1990s
Series notes: Besides this novel, King's Kate Martinelli series consists of *A Grave Talent* (1993—Edgar Award and John Creasey Dagger winner), *With Child* (1996—Edgar Award nomination), and *Night Work* (2000).

Subject headings: The Bible; Fools; Homeless; Shakespeare, William

Appeal points: This is one of the most inventive characters in mystery fiction. Because the book plays with the conventions of the genre, it should appeal to people who liked other mysteries that stepped out of the fold, like Josephine Tey's *The Daughter of Time*.

Readalikes

George Dawes Green's *The Caveman's Valentine*—similar use of challenged character

Mark Haddon's *The Curious Incident of the Dog in the Night-Time*—similar use of challenged character

Claire McNab's Carol Ashton series—similar use of challenged character

DISCUSSION QUESTIONS

How tough a cop is Kate Martinelli?

How would you rate Kate and Al as partners?

How does her sexual orientation add to her difficulties making it in a man's world?

How would you rate Kate and Lee as partners?

How guilty should Kate feel about Lee?

What should society do with people like Brother Erasmus?

How should Kate help David Sawyer?

What should society do with movements like the Holy Fools?

See standard questions in the Introduction for more questions.

◇◇◆◇◇

Margaret K. Lawrence

Hearts and Bones

Margaret Keilstrup was born in 1945 in Fremont, Nebraska. She has a degree from Midland College and a Ph.D. from the University of Nebraska. She has spent time as a translator, singer, artist, designer, and instructor at the university level. Margaret was a scriptwriter for the television show *The Equalizer*. Under the pseudonym M. K. Lorens, she has written the Winston Marlow Sherman mystery series.

Web site:
none
Reader's guide:
none

Plot summary: Three years after the end of the Revolutionary War, the people in the small town of Rufford, Maine, are struggling to regain balance and to integrate the soldiers who fought to establish a new nation back into their community. One of those soldiers is Major Daniel Josselyn, one of the town's wealthiest men. When midwife Hannah Trevor discovers the raped and strangled corpse of Anthea Emory, the town begins to collapse in on itself. One of three accused is Josselyn, the rumored father of Hannah's deaf eight-year-old daughter Jennet.

Publication date: 1996
Number of pages: 307
Geographic setting: Maine, Rufford; Maine, Webb's Ford
Time period: 1780s
Series notes: Besides this novel, Hannah Trevor appears in *Blood Red Roses* (1998), *The Burning Bride* (1999), and *Iceweaver* (2000).

Subject headings: Deaf; Midwives; U.S. Revolution, 1775–1783

Readalikes

Laurie R. King's Mary Russell series—similar use of historical setting

Appeal points: This novel was nominated for the Agatha, Anthony, Edgar, and Macavity awards for best novel.

DISCUSSION QUESTIONS

How did the author use diary entries, trial reports, recipes and her narrative to establish an atmosphere?

What details about this time period do you remember from the story?

What specific problems in this novel can be related to the aftereffects of the Revolution? Has life changed for the residents since they obtained their freedom?

Is Hannah scorned for her own independence or is she being punished for the Loyalist beliefs of her missing husband James?

Rape is a heinous act and a powerful symbol in this novel. How many women are affected by these acts?

Does the story of William Quaid explain his actions?

What separates a woman like Hannah from women today?

What hope is there for a woman like Hannah, or a child like Jennet?

See standard questions in the Introduction for more questions.

◇◇◆◇◇

John Le Carré

The Spy Who Came in from the Cold

David John Moore Cornwell was born in Poole, Dorsetshire, England, in 1931. He attended Bern University from 1948 until 1949 and taught middle school in Glastonbury from 1954 to 1955. In 1956 he received a B.A. from Lincoln College, Oxford. From 1956 to 1958, Cornwell was a tutor at Eton College. He later served as the British Foreign Office's second secretary in Bonn, West Germany (1960–1963), and as British consul in Hamburg, West Germany (1963–1964).

Cornwell had also joined the British Army Intelligence Corps in 1949, and until the 1960s, he worked at various times for them, using his other jobs as cover. He was required by his service in the intelligence corps to adopt a pseudonym for his fiction writing. Le Carré's non-Smiley novels are *The Looking-Glass War* (1965), *A Small Town in Germany* (1968), *The Naive and Sentimental Lover* (1971), *The Honourable Schoolboy* (1977), *The Little Drummer Girl* (1983), *A Perfect Spy* (1986), *The Russia House* (1989), *The Secret Pilgrim* (1991), *The Night Manager* (1993), *Our Game* (1995), and *The Tailor of Panama* (1996). He was made a Grand Master by the Mystery Writers of America in 1986 and received the Diamond Dagger award for lifetime achievement from the Crime Writers' Association. He was married twice and has four children. He lives in London and Cornwall, England.

Web site:
none
Reader's guide:
none

Plot summary: Alec Leamas is a British agent in Berlin, Germany. He is the control for double agents in East Germany, but someone has started to murder his people. London wants Leamas to go undercover, disguised as a disgraced spy, and discover where the leak has developed in the organization. What Leamas discovers is that he is a pawn to be used by both sides, and he must play one against the other in order to survive.

Publication date: 1965
Number of pages: 256
Geographic setting: East Germany, East Berlin
Time period: 1960s
Series notes: The George Smiley novels are *Call for the Dead* (1961), *A Murder of Quality (1962), Tinker, Tailor, Soldier, Spy (1974)*, and *Smiley's People* (1980), and he is a minor character in a number of others including this title.

Subject headings: Communism; Espionage

Appeal points: This novel won the Edgar Award, the Gold Dagger Award, and the Somerset Maugham Award. It will work in a novel-

Readalikes

Eric Ambler's *A Coffin for Dimitrios*—similar use of plot and character

Graham Greene—similar sense of style

into-film discussion. Because of Le Carré's service in the intelligence business, his novel has an air of authority and authenticity. Due to the melancholy nature of this story, it is hard to find a hero in the tale.

DISCUSSION QUESTIONS

How does this novel differ from Ian Fleming's novels about James Bond?

Leamas is asked to play the role of a dishonored spy, but how far is he from the truth when he accepts the part?

Why does Leamas not tell Control he wants to quit and not leave the safety of London?

Control is aptly named. How much control does Leamas have on this assignment?

If there is no moral code in the business of spying, why does Leamas feel so bad?

Why is it fair for those of us who stay home to expect people like Leamas to do what they do?

Leamas complains to Liz that in her country everything is about "sacrificing the individual to the mass." Is his country much different?

Which side of this conflict is right?

Does Fiedler deserve his fate?

Does Mundt deserve his fate?

What tragic flaw makes Leamas care about Liz and place himself in danger?

What is the author trying to tell us with the tragic end to Liz and Leamas?

See standard questions in the Introduction for more questions.

◇◇◆◇◇

Harper Lee

To Kill a Mockingbird

Nelle Harper Lee was born in 1926 in Monroeville, Alabama, the daughter of a lawyer and a homemaker. She attended grade school with Truman Capote, who became the model for Dill in this novel. After graduating from Huntingdon College, she studied law at the University of Alabama and spent one year at Oxford University. In the 1950s she worked as an airline reservation clerk in New York City, until she wrote this novel. It is her only published novel. She also contributed some articles to *Vogue* and *McCall's* magazines. She divides her time between New York City and Monroeville.

Web site:
http://mockingbird.chebucto.org/index.html

Reader's guide:
http://www.yabookscentral.com/cfusion/index.cfm?fuseAction=guides.guide&guide_id=45&book_id=143

Readalikes

Thomas H. Cook's *Breakheart Hill*—similar use of plot and character

Thomas H. Cook's *The Chatham School Affair*—similar use of plot and character

David Guterson's *Snow Falling on Cedars*—similar coming-of-age story

Plot summary: Jean "Scout" Finch tells us the story of her hometown of Maycomb, Alabama. Over a three-year period, she details the consequences of her lawyer father Atticus Finch's decision to defend a black man, Tom Robinson. Robinson has been accused of raping a white woman named Mavella Ewell. Scout, her brother Jem, and their friend Dill Harris have many coming-of-age experiences over the course of the novel, including witnessing the racial prejudice of their small town and the mystery of their neighborhood boogeyman, "Boo" Radley.

Publication date: 1960
Number of pages: 323
Geographic setting: Alabama, Maycomb
Time period: 1930s
Series notes: This is a stand-alone novel.
Subject headings: African Americans; Coming of age; Courtroom dramas; Race relations; Rape; The South
Appeal points: This novel was a Pulitzer Prize winner. It can be used for a novel-into-film discussion.

DISCUSSION QUESTIONS

What elements of this novel make it unique to its setting?

What elements of this novel would have to change in order for this story to happen in your hometown?

Do you think Bob Ewell is typical of the residents of Maycomb, or is he an anomaly?

What is the point of Jem's experiences with Mrs. Dubose?

What is meant by the fact that the Finch family has Calpurnia, a black housekeeper?

Scout rejects book learning. How is she "taught" in this novel, if not in school?

What does Alexandria want for the children that sets her apart from her brother?

Does it change your reading of this novel if you know that Dill is based on Lee's friend, Truman Capote?

How does this novel maintain the idea that it is narrated by a child?

Who is the mockingbird?

Why does the jury find Tom guilty?

Why is it important that Atticus be skilled enough with a gun to kill a rabid dog?

Did Atticus' effort make a difference?

What makes Boo Radley the way he is?

Why does Boo save Scout from Bob Ewell?

Does Atticus make the right decision about Boo?

If the children can understand Boo, why cannot the town of Maycomb understand Tom?

Does this novel make all black characters noble and all poor white characters trash?

Despite the novel's rather grim story, there is humor in this book. What made you laugh in this novel?

See standard questions in the Introduction for more questions.

◇◇◆◇◇

Dennis Lehane

Mystic River

Dennis Lehane was born in 1965 in Dorchester, Massachusetts, the son of a factory foreman and a school cafeteria worker. He earned a B.A.S. from Eckerd College in 1988 and an M.F.A. from the Florida International University in 1993. Lehane has taught mentally handicapped children, taught English, and worked as a chauffeur. He created the series about private eye characters Patrick Kenzie and Angela Gennaro in 1994 with *A Drink before the War,* winner of the Shamus Award for best first private eye novel of the year. These novels were followed by *Darkness, Take My Hand* (1996), *Sacred* (1998), *Gone, Baby, Gone* (1999), and *Prayers for Rain* (2000). After *Mystic River,* he wrote a second stand-alone novel, *Shutter Island* (2003). Lehane received the Shamus Award for the best first novel of the year 1994 for *A Drink before the War.*

Web site:
none
Reader's guide:
none

Plot summary: Twenty-five years prior to the main action of this novel, three childhood friends in a blue-collar Boston neighborhood are playing on the street when one makes the mistake of getting into the car of a pedophile. Disappearing for four days, the young boy returns to grow up in his neighborhood. In the main action of the book, the lives of the three men now intersect when one man's daughter is murdered, one friend is the investigator, and one is the chief suspect in the case.

Publication date: 2001
Number of pages: 401
Geographic setting: Massachusetts, Boston, East Buckingham
Time period: 1970s, 1990s
Series notes: This is a stand-alone novel.

Subject headings: Children at risk; Coming of age; Friendship

Appeal points: Mystic River was a finalist for the L. L. Winship/ PEN New England Award and the winner of the Anthony Award for Best Novel. It will make a great novel-into-film discussion title. The compelling story of these characters, displayed across this blue-collar neighborhood, should appeal to all readers.

Readalikes

Elizabeth Inness-Brown's *Burning Marguerite*—similar use of time as a theme

S. J. Rozan's *Absent Friends*—similar use of time as a theme

DISCUSSION QUESTIONS

Are books about the death of children too painful to read?

Did East Buckingham create this crime?

Why is the young Dave everyone's target before he gets into the car?

Jimmy complains that minor decisions change your life. How would his life have been different if he had gotten into that car?

How different would Dave's life be if he had not gotten into the car?

Why has Dave never gotten over the four missing days from his childhood?

Why does the author choose to make Dave a high-school baseball star?

In the park, is Jimmy wrong to react the way he did?

On page 56, Celeste sees something in Dave's eyes. What do you think it was?

What can society do to give children like Brendan and Silent Ray a chance?

How does this novel work as a straight mystery? Did you know who had killed Kate?

Is Dave guilty enough to be executed by Jimmy?

What should Sean do to Jimmy at the end of the novel?

See standard questions in the Introduction for more questions.

◇◇◆◇◇

Donna Leon

Death at La Fenice

Donna Leon was born in 1942 in New Jersey. A former teacher, Leon has lived in Switzerland, Saudi Arabia, Iran, and China. She currently lives in Venice, Italy. Her novel *Friends in High Places* won the Crime Writers' Association Macallan Silver Dagger for Fiction.

Web site:
http://www.groveatlantic.com/leon/leon.htm

Reader's guide:
none

Plot summary: World famous German conductor Helmut Wellauer has been found dead backstage at the Venetian opera house, La Fenice. Called to the scene for his first case in print is police commissario Guido Brunetti. Clues abound as the detective discovers the conductor was not a nice man, his wife is indifferent to his death, and the homosexuals who work in his profession often faced his scorn. While Brunetti attacks this case intellectually, his irritating supervisor calls for action. The politics of modern Venice and the social life and customs of its residents are displayed, as well as the interesting but equally frustrating home life of a working-class father. Eventually the book concludes with a tragic tale foreshadowed by the clues, yet still surprising when it is delivered.

Publication date: 1992

Number of pages: 278

Geographic setting: Italy, Venice

Time period: 1990s

Series notes: There are now twelve books in the series about Brunetti. After this title, they are *Death in a Strange Country* (1993), *Dressed for Death* (also: *The Anonymous Venetian*) (1994), *Death and Judgment* (1995), *Acqua Alta* (1996), *The Death of Faith* (also: *Quietly in Their Sleep*) (1997), *A Noble Radiance* (1998), *Fatal Remedies* (1999), *Friends in High Places* (2000), *Uniform Justice* (2003), *Doctored Evidence* (2004), and *Blood from a Stone* (2005).

Subject heading: Opera

Appeal points: This novel won the Suntory Prize (Japan) for best suspense novel. Probably the greatest appeal of this novel is its excellent use of the local color. However, its most winning attraction is the wry and witty way it examines the Italian culture and the people who populate this fascinating sea-city.

Readalikes

Cara Black's Amiee Le Duc series—similar setting

Michael Didbin's Aurelio Zen series—similar setting

Jan-Willem Van de Wetering's Rinus DeGier, Rinus and Henk Grijpstra series—similar use of character

DISCUSSION QUESTIONS

What particular things do you remember that you would say are Venetian?

What techniques does commissario Brunetti use to manipulate people?

Why do Count Falier and Brunetti dislike each other?

How would you describe Brunetti's style as a detective?

How good a detective is Brunetti?

What made Wellauer the nasty piece of work he appears to be?

What would make Elizabeth fall in love with Wellauer?

Was taking away Wellauer's music a "fair" trade?

After Wellauer's death, Brunetti says L'Unita's editorial calls for "vengeance, which, predictably, it had got confused with justice." Why are these not the same?

How does Brunetti manage to reach the point where the laws of the state are balanced against more "humane" laws?

Can society survive if policemen believe "what we think is right isn't the same as what the law says is right" (p. 131)?

Does Brunetti make the right choice at the end of the novel?

See standard questions in the Introduction for more questions.

◇◇◆◇◇

Elmore Leonard

Get Shorty

Elmore Leonard was born in 1925 in New Orleans, Louisiana. He served in the Naval Reserve from 1943 until 1946. In 1950 Leonard earned a B.A. from the University of Detroit. He worked as a copywriter from 1950 until 1961, then worked freelance until 1963. From 1963 until 1966 he ran his own advertising company. Leonard has been a full-time writer since 1967.

Leonard's first novel, *The Bounty Hunter*, was published in 1953. Originally a Western writer, he turned to crime fiction. His first crime novel, rejected eighty-four times, was published as a Gold Medal paperback called *The Big Bounce* in 1969. The Western Writers of America listed *Hombre* (1961) as one of the best twenty-five western novels of all time. *La Brava* won the Edgar Award in 1984. The Hammett Award was given to *Maximum Bob* in 1991. Leonard was declared a Grand Master by the Mystery Writers of America in 1992. Leonard has also authored numerous screenplays. He married three times and has five children.

Web site:
http://www.elmoreleonard.com
Reader's guide:
none

Plot summary: Chili Palmer is a Miami loan shark in pursuit of a deadbeat who is headed to Vegas with his boss's money. Then Chili finds himself in Hollywood where he meets a washed-up B-movie producer named Harry Zimm and an out-of-work actress named Karen Flores who is willing to listen to his patter. Chili decides to produce a movie. But first he will have to deal with some really angry cocaine dealers and loan sharks.

Publication date: 1990

Number of pages: 292

Geographic setting: California, Los Angeles; Florida, Miami; Nevada, Las Vegas

Time period: 1990s

Series notes: Chili Palmer also appears in *Be Cool* (1999).

Subject headings: Gangsters; Hollywood

Readalikes

Laurence Shames—similar use of character and plot

Charlie Stella—similar use of character and plot

Appeal points: This novel works well in a novel-into-film discussion. There are only anti-heroes in the books of Elmore Leonard, and this does not appeal to all readers. In addition, the situations and the language can be too rough for some readers. The power of Leonard's style is his use of dialog and humor to tell his story.

DISCUSSION QUESTIONS

What are some of the funniest things you remember about this story?

What is the moral center of this book? How do we justify rooting for a mobster?

Can you think of some examples of how Leonard used dialog to project his story?

Can you identify the code by which Chili lives his life?

Can you explain how any Hollywood films get made if they are made by men like Zimm?

In the future, what will people learn about the 1990s by reading this novel?

Is any justice served in this novel?

See standard questions in the Introduction for more questions.

◇◇◆◇◇

Laura Lippman

Every Secret Thing

Laura Lippman was born in Atlanta, Georgia, the daughter of a journalist and a children's librarian. Her family moved to Baltimore in 1965. Lippman earned a B.A. in journalism from Northwestern University. Lippman began her journalism career as a reporter for the *Waco Herald-Tribune* in 1981 and then moved to the *San Antonio Light* in 1983. She began work for the *Baltimore Sun* as a reporter in 1989. Her Tess Monaghan private detective series includes *Baltimore Blues* (1997—nominated for the Shamus Award for Best First Novel), *Charm City* (1997—Edgar and Shamus award winner for best paperback original), *Butcher's Hill* (1998—nominated for an Edgar and a Shamus and winner of the Agatha Award for best paperback original), *In Big Trouble* (1999), *The Sugar House* (2000), *In a Strange City* (2001), *Last Place* (2002), and *By a Spider's Thread* (2004—Agatha and Edgar Award nominations). Her other stand-alone novel is *To the Power of Three* (2005). Lippman lives in Baltimore, Maryland.

Plot summary: Two eleven-year-old girls, banished from a party, decide to take an unprotected child they find on a Baltimore porch. When four days go by and the child is found dead, the case is resolved with the arrest of the two girls, Alice Manning and Ronnie Fuller. The courts send the children away for seven years, quieting the racial tension aroused because the girls are white and the dead child is black. Seven years later, the two girls are released from juvenile detention and return to their old neighborhood, where the mother of the dead child, a judge's daughter named Cynthia Barnes, still lives. When other children begin to disappear, the case is assigned to county homicide cop Nancy Porter, a woman with a mystical connection to the previous murder.

Web site:
http://www.lauralippman.com/index.html

Reader's guide:
none

Readalikes

Thomas H. Cook's *Red Leaves*—similar use of plot and character

Reginald Hill's *On Beulah Height*—similar use of plot and character

Dennis Lehane's *Mystic River*—similar use of plot

Val McDermid's *A Place of Execution*—similar use of plot and character

Publication date: 2003
Number of pages: 388
Geographic setting: Maryland, Baltimore
Time period: 1990s, 2000s
Series notes: This is a stand-alone novel.
Subject heading: Children at risk
Appeal points: This novel won the Anthony and Barry awards for best novel of the year. With the painful display of the impending new tragedy layered on top of the horrifying previous crime, this novel has a sense of inevitability about it that reminds readers of

the slow descent of a horror story. Although disturbing to read, the story is artfully told and appeals to crime novel readers who like to be chilled.

DISCUSSION QUESTIONS

Does Nancy, "the goddess of small things," get lost in the details?

Is Sharon a fulfilled woman?

Why does the world need people like Rosario Bustamante?

What does Mira need?

What would have made Alice different as a child and steered her away from the crime?

Why is Alice fat?

How guilty is Helen in creating the Alice who goes to prison the first time? How guilty is Helen for Alice's actions the second time?

What are the differences between Alice and Ronnie?

What keeps Ronnie from recovery?

What does it mean that only Ronnie can cut herself?

Why does Ronnie commit suicide?

How should juvenile murderers be treated by the courts?

See standard questions in the Introduction for more questions.

Peter Lovesey

The Detective Wore Silk Drawers

Peter Lovesey was born in 1936 in Whitton, Middlesex, England, the son of a bank official. Lovesey earned a B.A. from the University of Reading in 1958. From 1958 until 1961, he served in the Royal Air Force. He married Jacqueline Lewis in 1959, and they have three children. From 1961 until 1975, Lovesey worked in the education field. His first novel was *Wobble to Death* (1970), which introduced Cribb and Thackery. He has a contemporary series about a detective named Peter Diamond and numerous stand-alone crime novels.

He won the Gold Dagger Award for *The False Inspector Dew* (1982), an Edgar nomination for *Rough Cider* (1986), an Edgar nomination and a Silver Dagger award for *The Summons* (1995), and a Silver Dagger award for Bloodhounds (1996).

> **Web site:**
> none
> **Reader's guide:**
> none

Plot summary: Victorian-age pugilism forms the background for this novel featuring Sergeant Cribb. A headless corpse is disposed in the Thames, and the police link it to Radstock Hall, where it is believed that illegal bare-knuckled boxers are trained. The police send in undercover Constable Jago because he is the police boxing champion. Prepared to face fists in the ring, Jago is not prepared to meet the powerful and seductive Isabel Vibart.

Publication date: 1971

Number of pages: 188

Geographic setting: England, London

Time period: 1870s

Series notes: The first novel in this series, *Wobble to Death* (1970), was selected for the Macmillan/Panther First Crime Novel award. Additional novels in the series are *Abracadaver* (1972), *Mad Hatter's Holiday: A Novel of Murder in Victorian Brighton* (1973), *Invitation to a Dynamite Party* (1974; also: *The Tick of Death*), *A Case of Spirits* (1975), *Swing, Swing Together* (1976), and *Waxwork* (1978).

Subject headings: Boxing; Gambling; Victorian England

Appeal points: The author successfully portrays the Victorian period for the reader. Jago, in a one book supporting role as an undercover detective, enhances the appeal of the series characters.

> **Readalikes**
>
> Ray Harrison's Joseph Bragg and James Morton series—similar use of historical settings and character
>
> Anne Perry's Thomas and Charlotte Pitt series—similar use of historical settings and character
>
> Francis Selwyn's Sergeant Verity series—similar use of historical settings and character

DISCUSSION QUESTIONS

How does the author make Victorian Age boxing come alive for the reader?

Is it fair for men like Jago to place themselves in dangerous undercover operations?

How culpable is Cribb for what happens to Jago?

What role does Isabel Vibart play in the novel?

Is she an understandable femme fatale or a male fantasy figure?

What separates Lydia from Isabel?

See standard questions in the Introduction for more questions.

◇◇◀▶◇◇

Henning Mankell

Faceless Killers

Henning Mankell was born in Sweden in 1948. His first writing experience was as a playwright, and his first novel was published in 1973. His nonseries book, *The Return of the Dancing Master*, published in 2000, stars a detective named Stefan Lindman. Mankell has also written children's books. He splits his time between his home in Sweden and Maputo, Mozambique, where he is the director of the Teatro Avenida.

Plot summary: In the frozen province of Skåne, Sweden, an elderly farmer is murdered in his farmhouse. Inspector Kurt Wallander is assigned to the case. His first and only clue is the dying word spoken by the farmer's wife, "Foreigner." As racial tension builds in the region and a death occurs, pressure is put on Wallander to solve the crime. Rejected by his father, wife, and daughter, Wallander lives a lonely and isolated life, not unlike the landscape across which he is chasing a killer.

Web site:
http://www.inspector-wallander.org

Reader's guide:
http://www.readinggroupguides
.com/guides3/faceless_killers1.asp

Publication date: 1991
Number of pages: 284
Geographic setting: Sweden, Skåne, Lunnarp Village; Sweden, Skåne, Ystad
Time period: 1990s
Series notes: This is the first novel in the Kurt Wallander series. The rest of the books are *The Dogs of Riga* (1992), *The White Lioness* (1993), *The Man Who Smiled* (1994), *Sidetracked* (1995), *The Fifth Woman* (1996), *One Step Behind* (1997), *Firewall* (1998), *The Pyramid* (1999—a collection of short stories), *Before the Frost* (Linda Wallander's case) (2002), and *The Grave* (2004).
Subject headings: Hate groups; Race relations

Appeal points: North American readers will find a sensibility in the style of Mankell that appeals to those looking for an examination of a different culture. Wallander is a wounded character, and his struggles with his shortcomings engage readers who like their main characters flawed.

Readalikes

Maj Sjowall and Per Wahloo's Martin Beck series—similar use of style, character, and setting

DISCUSSION QUESTIONS

Are all cultures doomed to have a fear of foreigners?

What was the impact of the weather on the mood of the book?

Why is a rural murder scarier than an urban crime?

Why do many authors have their police detectives unhappily wed?

What images of Sweden do you remember from this book?

What should Wallander do about his father?

What does Wallander need?

Who is the black woman in Wallander's dream?

Why did Linda leave home at the age of fifteen?

Wallander claims that "a new world had emerged, and he hadn't even noticed it." What changes in his country are similar to those you see in your own?

Wallander says he will take seven days off from work and "emerge a new man." What hope do you hold out for the success of this effort?

See standard questions in the Introduction for more questions.

◇◇◆◇◇

Margaret Maron

Bootlegger's Daughter

Margaret Maron was born in Greensboro, North Carolina. In 1959 she dropped out of college to marry Joseph J. Maron, whom she met while working at the Pentagon. They have one child, and the couple has lived in Italy and New York. Her series about New York cop Sigrid Harald includes *One Coffee With* (1981), *Death of a Butterfly* (1984), *Death in Blue Folders* (1985), *The Right Jack* (1987), *Baby Doll Games* (1988), *Corpus Christmas* (1989—Agatha and Anthony nomination), *Past Imperfect* (1991), and *Fugitive Colors* (1995). Her short story, *The Dog that Didn't Bark*, won an Agatha Award in 2003.

Web site:
http://www.margaretmaron.com
Reader's guide:
none

Plot summary: Lawyer Deborah Knott, a native girl with family roots deep in the area, decides to run for the Colleton County judgeship. At the same time, she begins to investigate an eighteen-year-old mystery. Gayle Whitehead never knew her mother Janie, who was murdered when Gayle was a baby. Now, as she approaches adulthood, Gayle wants the mystery of her mother's death explained. No one expects this investigation to lead to new murders and expose the underbelly of this community.

Publication date: 1993
Number of pages: 261
Geographic setting: North Carolina, Colleton County, Cotton Grove
Time period: 1990s
Series notes: This is the first book in the series. Others are *Southern Discomfort* (1993—Agatha and Anthony nomination), *Shooting at Loons* (1994), *Up Jumps the Devil* (1996—Anthony Award winner for best novel), *Killer Market* (1997), *Home Fires* (1998), *Storm Track* (2000—Agatha Award winner for best novel), *Uncommon Clay* (2001), *Slow Dollar* (2002), *High Country Fall* (2004—Agatha Award nomination), and *Rituals of the Season* (2005).
Subject headings: Elections; Homosexuality; Lawyers

Readalikes

Donna Andrews' Meg Langslow series—similar use of character

Janet Evanovich's Stephanie Plum series—similar use of character

Appeal points: This novel won all four major mystery awards: the Agatha, Anthony, Edgar, and Macavity. One of the huge appeals of this book is the eccentric and loveable Southern family life on display in this book and the rest of the series titles. Readers may find the character of Deborah Knott unique with her quirky and appealing style.

DISCUSSION QUESTIONS

Can you identify things in this book that are particularly Southern?

How much is to be made of the fact that Deb is the daughter of a bootlegger?

How loyal should Deb be to her family?

What purpose does the election serve in this novel?

What role does Michael Vickery play in this tale?

Is homosexuality to blame for this crime?

Why does Gayle really need to know what happened to her mother?

Does the truth help or hurt Gayle?

See standard questions in the Introduction for more questions.

◇◇◆◇◇

Ngaio Marsh

Vintage Murder

Edith Ngaio (Nye-O) Marsh was born in Merivale, New Zealand, in 1895. She attended St. Margaret's College from 1910 to 1913 and Canterbury University School of Art from 1914 until 1919. From 1919 to 1923, she toured Australia and New Zealand as a member of the Allan Wilkie Shakespeare Company and with other companies. From 1923 to 1927, Marsh was a theater producer. She moved to London in 1928, staying till 1932, working as an interior decorator. From 1933 until her death, she lived in London and Christchurch, working as a full-time writer and as a producer of plays. During World War II, she served as a Red Cross ambulance driver. She was given the Dame Commander, Order of the British Empire, in 1966. In 1977, the Mystery Writers of America made her a Grand Master. Marsh died in 1982 in Christchurch, New Zealand. Her autobiography, *Black Beech and Honeydew*, was published in 1965.

Web site:
none
Reader's guide:
none

Plot summary: Roderick Alleyn of Scotland Yard is vacationing in New Zealand and traveling by train when he meets the members of the Caroline Dacres English Comedy Company. A hint of things to come occurs when Alfred Meyer claims someone tried to push him off the train as the Chief Detective Inspector travels with the troop. Later Alleyn witnesses the murder of Alfred Meyer, caused by a champagne bottle used as a stunt during a celebration, and decides to lend a hand to the local police investigation.

Publication date: 1937
Number of pages: 275
Geographic setting: New Zealand, Middleton
Time period: 1930s
Series notes: There are thirty-two novels in this series, of which this title is the fifth.
Subject heading: Maori; Theater
Appeal points: This is a Golden Age puzzle, and the appeal will be in trying to solve the crime. Readers who also enjoy the arts should find the theater setting interesting.

Readalikes

Margery Allingham—similar use of character

Agatha Christie—similar use of plot

Ellery Queen's *The Roman Hat Mystery*—similar use of plot

Dorothy Sayers—similar use of character

DISCUSSION QUESTIONS

What characteristics does Roderick Alleyn display that make him a classic detective? What characteristics does he have that make him different from other Golden Age detectives?

Because this is a Golden Age novel, the puzzle is the book. Did this mystery mystify? Were there enough clues to help you solve the crime?

Considering he is not on his home turf, how did Alleyn do as a detective in a foreign land?

How does Marsh manage to create a closed set of characters for her mystery?

What did you learn about the theater from this novel?

How did the author effectively use the New Zealand setting?

What things in this book did you find humorous?

See standard questions in the Introduction for more questions.

◇◇◆◇◇

J(ulia) Wallis Martin

Julia Wallis Martin was born in 1957. Her mother left her father and through a series of affairs and bad marriages, tried to raise Julia. Depressed and addicted to pills, Julia's mother attempted suicide. She eventually died of cancer when her daughter was seventeen. Wallis Martin moved to Oxford, where she worked as a waitress and had one short story published. At the age of twenty she was tragically widowed when her first husband, Terry Flahery, was killed in an automobile accident. She has a son, James, from that marriage. At age twenty-seven, she married a man who took her to South Africa, where she lived for seven years and worked as an editor in a publishing house. Her marriage ended when violence in the country drove her and her son back to England without her husband. Her novel, *A Likeness in Stone*, was published in 1998 under the name J. Wallis Martin. All of the following novels have been published under the name Julia Wallis Martin: *The Bird Yard* (1999), *The Long Close Call* (2000), and *Dancing with the Uninvited Guest* (2002). She is now married to screenwriter Russell Murray, and they live in a cottage in Somerset, England.

Web site:
http://www.gregoryandcompany.
co.uk/pages/authors/index.asp?
AuthorID=37

Reader's guide:
none

The Bird Yard

Plot summary: Based on a childhood memory from her days of living on a council estate, Wallis Martin presents a home turned into an aviary, surrounded by wire yet full of the color and song of finches. In the neighborhood where the Bird Yard lies, a young boy named Gary Maudsley has disappeared, echoing a pattern from five years earlier when a young boy named Joseph Coyne also went missing. Detective Superintendent Parker sees the pattern, sees the aviary, and works hard to draw a straight line from one to the other. With the help of profiler Murray Hanson, the detective tries to keep his own paternal feelings intact as he struggles to be objective on this aggravating and intense case of murder.

Readalikes

Dennis Lehane's *Mystic River*—similar use of plot

Val McDermid's *A Place of Execution*—similar use of plot

Ruth Rendell—similar use of psychological suspense

Minette Walters—similar use of psychological suspense

Publication date: 1999
Number of pages: 340
Geographic setting: England, Manchester
Time period: 1990s
Series notes: This is a stand-alone novel.
Subject headings: Children at risk; Pedophilia

Appeal points: Hard to say that a novel about child abuse and pedophilia has appeal, but it can be said that the strength of this title relies on the ability of the author to psychologically thrill the reader.

DISCUSSION QUESTIONS

Did you like the style of this book?

How were you affected by the imagery of the birds?

Can you name some examples of foreshadowing using birds?

Did you like Parker?

What do you know about Parker?

Is it important to be able to identify with the hero?

Who is the bigger hero: Bennett or Parker?

Did you like Hanson?

What do you know about Hanson?

Could you forgive Hanson?

Did you like Brogan Healy?

What do you know about Brogan?

What is Brogan's fate?

What monsters are scarier: a Hannibal Lecture (see everything) or a Roly (see nothing)?

What was the role of the women characters in this book? Maureen the cop/Jan/Lorna/Julie Coyne/Elaine

What is the fate of the weak in our world?

Can we fireproof our children?

What is it about children in jeopardy that makes it so hard to read about?

See standard questions in the Introduction for more questions.

◇◇◆◇◇

A Likeness in Stone

Plot summary: A reservoir has flooded an area where a murder has been committed, and twenty years later when a diver uncovers a corpse hidden in a submerged house, it confirms the worst fears of retired Thames Valley Chief

Inspector Bill Driver. He now knows where the body of Helena Warner has rested all these years. His new mission becomes revisiting her three friends who years ago, as undergraduates, hid the truth from the investigator.

Publication date: 1998

Number of pages: 280

Geographic setting: England, Marshfield; England, Oxford

Time period: 1970s, 1990s

Series notes: This is a stand-alone novel.

Subject headings: Oxford University; Reservoirs

Appeal points: The novel was a Barry and Edgar nominee for best novel of the year. Across time, the story of the four students should have compelling appeal to all readers.

Readalikes

Reginald Hill's *On Beulah Height*—similar use of plot

Peter Robinson's *In a Dry Season*—similar use of plot

DISCUSSION QUESTIONS

What does it tell us about these three people if they can keep a secret for twenty years?

Why does Driver still care after twenty years?

What were Joan Poole's motivations for her actions twenty years ago?

What are her motivations now?

What does it tell us if a man like Richard Wachman is also a great artist?

What can be done to help Ian Gilmore after Wachman confesses?

If Gilmore had confessed twenty years ago, would Driver have probed on to get to the real truth that took twenty years to reveal?

How guilty are the Wachmans for not taking care of their son?

Is any case ever "as simple as that"?

See standard questions in the Introduction for more questions.

◇◇◆◇◇

Alexander McCall Smith

The No. 1 Ladies' Detective Agency

Alexander McCall Smith was born in 1948 in the British colony of Southern Rhodesia (now Zimbabwe). McCall Smith studied law in Scotland and became a professor of medical law at Edinburgh University. Later, he taught law at the University of Botswana, where he helped write the country's criminal code. McCall Smith served as vice chairman of the Human Genetics Commission of the United Kingdom for UNESCO. He has written over fifty books, including works on medical ethics and criminal law, fiction, short stories, and works specifically for children. His favorite occupation is playing the bassoon (badly) in the Really Terrible Orchestra. He lives in Edinburgh, is married to Elizabeth, and they have two daughters.

Web site:
http://www.randomhouse.com/
features/mccallsmith

Reader's guide:
http://www.randomhouse.
com/features/mccallsmith/books_
ladies_rgg.html

Plot summary: This novel has a unique and interesting style as it approaches the life and times of "Mma" Precious Ramotswe, Botswana's only private detective. Episodic by design, it reads almost like a collection of interrelated short stories. It moves across time, and shifts point of view, to reveal not only the nature of the individuals in this novel but also the underlying social and economic characteristics of this proud African country. While the book does not perform like a contemporary mystery, Precious must still solve various puzzles including a wandering daughter, a fake insurance claim, medical malpractice, and other ordinary concerns. But within the quiet revelations of the plot are also revealed the truths of this African nation: its language, culture, and religions. Broadcast over the arid surfaces of this fascinating country, Mma's detective skills allow her to display her concerns for the role of women in Botswanian society as well as the passionate love for an Africa not changed by Western ways.

Publication date: 1998

Number of pages: 226

Geographic setting: Botswana, Gaborone

Time period: 1990s

Series notes: This is the first novel in the series. The other books in the series are *Tears of the Giraffe* (2000), *Mortality for Beautiful Girls* (2001), *The Kalahari Typing School for Men* (2002), *The Full Cupboard of Life* (2003), and *In the Company of Cheerful Ladies* (2005).

Subject heading: Africa

Appeal points: *The No. 1 Ladies' Detective Agency* received two Booker Judges'

Readalikes

Agatha Christie's Jane Marple series—similar use of character

Dorothy Gilman—similar use of character

Baroness Orczy's *The Man in the Corner*—similar use of plot

Special Recommendations and was voted one of the International Books of the Year and the Millennium by the Times Literary Supplement. This title appeals to readers looking for a gentler read. McCall Smith's use of humor is another stand-out feature. The powerful presentation of this African landscape overwhelms the mystery stories that are told and the book appeals to readers who are not generally interested in reading detective fiction. Most readers are drawn to the unique nature of Mma, an extremely appealing character.

DISCUSSION QUESTIONS

How does this title differ from a typical mystery?

Does Precious remind you of any other detectives?

What qualities does Precious possess that make her a great detective?

Would you confess that your "cattle" are goats as Precious does as a young child? (p. 43)

Do you believe people "find out what was best for them, and then they would call that the right thing"? (p. 35)

Precious' father dies saying the words "but, but" when she tells him she will open a detective agency (p. 6). What do you think he was going to say?

McCall Smith, a white male, writes in the voice of an African woman. Does he get it right for you?

What sense of Botswana do you get from this book?

Botswana culture requires a family to take care of its members. Why, then, do you think there are still so many family problems?

How does the Patel family's Indian nature separate them from the average Botswana resident?

Was Jack real or imaginary when Precious convinces Mr. Patel to let his daughter Nandira live her life? (p. 12)

How does Precious' marriage to Note compare to Nandira's flirtation with Jack?

Do you agree with Precious' assessment of men?

What does "every man has a map in his heart of his own country" mean to you?

Why does Precious turn down the first proposal from Matekoni?

Why does she change her mind at the book's end?

See standard questions in the Introduction for more questions.

◇◇◆◇◇

Cormac McCarthy

No Country for Old Men

Charles McCarthy, named for his father, was born in 1933 in Providence, Rhode Island. His first name was legally changed to Cormac, which is Gaelic for "son of Charles." When he was four years old, his family moved to Knoxville, Tennessee. From 1951 to 1952 he attended the University of Tennessee. Subsequently, McCarthy served in the Air Force (1953–1956). Although he returned to the university after his military service, he left before completing a degree. He moved to Chicago, worked as an auto mechanic, and had a son, Cullen, from his marriage to Lee Holleman. They divorced prior to the beginning of his writing career. McCarthy has written the following novels: *The Orchard Keeper* (1965), *Outer Dark* (1968), *Child of God* (1974), *Suttree* (1979), *Blood Meridian, Or the Evening Redness in the West* (1985), *All the Pretty Horses* (1992), *The Crossing* (1994), and *Cities of the Plain* (1998). McCarthy received the National Book Award for fiction and the National Book Critics Award for fiction for *All the Pretty Horses*. He married Anne DeLisle in 1965 and divorced in 1978.

McCarthy moved to El Paso, Texas. He was married a third time in 1998 to his wife Jennifer; they have one child. They live in Santa Fe, New Mexico.

Web site:
http://www.cormacmccarthy.com
Reader's guide:
none

Plot summary: In all great noir stories, the lead character makes one fatal mistake. In this case, Llewelyn Moss decides to keep the $2 million in drug money that he stumbles on while hunting. Moss leaves behind the carnage of a drug deal gone bad, including the dead bodies of men on both sides of the deal. When the clues at the crime site lead Sheriff Ed Tom Bell to realize that Moss is in very deep trouble, he attempts to rescue him. Bell knows that both sides of the drug deal are after the money. One side sends an ex–Special Forces man. The other side sends a ghost: the extremely talented and dangerous psychotic Anton Chigruh. When everyone is done shooting each other, the key to the novel is who will survive this terrible killing field.

Publication date: 2005
Number of pages: 309
Geographic setting: Mexico; Texas
Time period: 1980s
Series notes: This is a stand-alone novel.
Subject heading: Drugs

Appeal points: This is a novel for those who enjoy the hardest of the hard-boiled style. Although it comes from a well-respected literary darling, its violence challenges many readers. That said, it is a scary look at how drugs have

Readalikes

James Lee Burke—similar use of theme
James Crumley—similar use of theme

ripped our society apart and changed the standard for human behavior. McCarthy's use of dialog to propel the narrative is masterful. This novel can promote discussion on the constant battle between good and evil.

DISCUSSION QUESTIONS

Did the author's choice of punctuation style help or hinder the story?

Should Moss have taken the money? Would you have taken the money?

Is Moss punished for not being a Good Samaritan when he abandons the dying man in the desert?

Why do you agree or disagree with this statement: "It takes very little to govern good people...and bad people can't be governed at all"?

What does Anton Chigruh want Carson Wells to say when he asks (p. 175), "If the rule you followed led you to this of what use was the rule?"

Moss says, "Things happen to you they happen...they don't require your permission." What has happened to free choice?

Chigruh says, "Somewhere you made a choice. All followed to this." Do choices we make predestine our lives?

Does this novel offer any hope?

See standard questions in the Introduction for more questions.

◇◇◆◇◇

Lise McClendon

One O'Clock Jump

Lise McClendon was born in 1952 in Carmel, California, and was raised in Delaware and Nebraska. Her father was a college botany professor and her mother was a cardiologist. McClendon received a B.A. in broadcast journalism and sociology from the University of Nebraska in 1974. In 1981 she earned an M.A. in communications from the University of Missouri—Kansas City. Since then, she has held a number of jobs in the communications business including a stint teaching broadcast journalism. She has written a series of mystery novels about art gallery owner Alix Thorssen, including *The Bluejay Shaman* (1994), *Painted Truth* (1995), *Nordic Nights* (1999), and *Blue Wolf* (2001). She lives in Billings, Montana, with her husband Kipp and two sons.

Plot summary: This historical mystery is set in the post-Pendergast period of Kansas City, Missouri, a town reeling from the effects of the Depression and the lack of control exhibited when social systems, even if they were corrupt, collapsed. Pendergast, the city's boss, has just

> **Web site:**
> http://www.lisemcclendon.com/homepage.html
> **Reader's guide:**
> none

gone to jail, and the city is in turmoil as others interested in the same graft and corruption fill the void he left. Amos Haddam is an Englishman with lungs damaged from mustard gas received in the trenches during World War I. He also has an unrequited ache for the love he lost at the same time, and he is trying to maintain the Sugar Moon Investigations agency with just one remaining operative: Dorie Lennox. Lennox is also damaged by the past, and her multiple defense mechanisms brought on by her previous troubles leave her remote and morose. But that damage has also made her tough as nails, and she is able to handle the pressures of an intense investigation launched in an air of secrecy and conspiracy. Lennox is given the job of tailing Iris Jackson by an unscrupulous lawyer and his mobbed-up client who claims Jackson is his girlfriend. Dorie is on the spot when Jackson commits suicide by jumping off one of the city's bridges late one night. Oddly, her client now wants her to continue to probe into the dead woman's life. As she does, she begins to suspect that her tail job was a phony, and so was the woman she was tailing.

Publication date: 2001
Number of pages: 276
Geographic setting: Missouri, Kansas City
Time period: 1930s
Series notes: The second book in this series is *Sweet and Lowdown*, published in 2002.

> **Readalikes**
>
> Sandra Scoppettone's *This Dame for Hire*—similar use of main character in a historical setting
>
> Jacqueline Winspear's series about Maisie Dobbs—similar use of main character in a historical setting

Subject heading: World War II

Appeal points: The echo of past occurrences reverberates throughout the work, with each major character damaged in some way by the past. The plot moves within the well-developed sense of both the historical and almost hysterical atmosphere of a dark, corrupt city teetering on the edge of control. The lead character should appeal to readers who like tough-talking, hard-boiled heroes.

DISCUSSION QUESTIONS

How did McClendon get the history right?

How tragic is the character of Amos?

Why does Dorie dislike being touched? Why does Dorie long to be a pilot? Why does Dorie hate rivers?

Do you think Dorie can ever have a normal relationship?

Is Dorie a good detective?

What is the meaning of Luther's story?

See standard questions in the Introduction for more questions.

◇◇◆◇◇

Sharyn McCrumb

If Ever I Return, Pretty Peggy-O

Sharyn Arrowood was born in 1948 in Wilmington, North Carolina. She earned a B.A. in communications and Spanish from the University of North Carolina in 1970. Sharyn worked various jobs in the education and journalism fields. She then earned an M.A. from Virginia Tech University. In 1982 she married David McCrumb; they have two children. She has been a full-time writer since 1988. Her first novel, *Sick of Shadows* (1984), introduces the series character Elizabeth MacPherson. Other titles in the MacPherson series are *Lovely in Her Bones* (1985), *Highland Laddie Gone* (1986), *Paying the Piper* (1988), *The Windsor Knot* (1990), *Missing Susan* (1991), *MacPherson's Lament* (1992), *If I'd Killed Him When I Met Him . . .* (1995—Agatha Award winner), and *The PMS Outlaws* (2000). Her Jay Omega Series includes *Bimbos of the Death Sun* (1988—Edgar Award winner) and *Zombies of the Gene Pool* (1992).

> **Web site:**
> http://www.sharynmccrumb.com
> **Reader's guide:**
> none

Plot summary: Hamelin High's class of 1966 is about to have their twentieth reunion. When 1960s folksinger Peggy Muryan moves to town, her hope is to have the peace and quiet she needs to compose new songs. Instead, she receives threatening messages and finds she needs the help of Sheriff Spencer Arrowood. Deputy Joe LeDonne begins to recognize references to Vietnam in the messages, and the cops have their first clue to follow when a woman who looks like Muryan is murdered.

Publication date: 1990

Number of pages: 312

Geographic setting: Tennessee, Hamelin

Time period: 1980s

Series notes: This novel is the first in a series of connected novels labeled The Ballad Series. The other novels are *The Hangman's Beautiful Daughter* (1992), *She Walks These Hills* (1994—Agatha, Anthony, Macavity, and Nero awards for best novel), *The Rosewood Casket* (1996), *Foggy Mountain Breakdown and Other Stories* (1997), *The Ballad of Frankie Silver* (1998), *The Song Catcher* (2000), *Ghost Riders* (2003), and *St. Dale* (2005).

Subject headings: Reunions; Veterans; Vietnamese Conflict, 1961–1975

Appeal points: This novel was a New York Times Notable Book and a Macavity Award winner for best novel. Because it is McCrumb's intent to write regional novels with serious historical and sociological aspects, the hope is that readers who do not like crime fiction will still like these novels.

> **Readalikes**
>
> Reginald Hill's *On Beulah Height*—similar use of plot
> Margaret Maron's Deborah Knott series—similar use of setting

DISCUSSION QUESTIONS

Does Martha get what she wants out of her reunion plans?

Do the women in this novel have a solid definition of what their role is in society?

How valuable are folksongs to future generations?

What attracts Spencer to Peggy?

Is Hamelin too bound to its old traditions?

How big a burden does Cal leave Spencer when he writes his last letter home?

How does the Vietnam experience still affect Hamelin?

Why is LeDonne able to function again in society while Roger struggles each day?

How much of the action of this novel can be dismissed to "the sins of the past"? How much responsibility do people have to get over the past and get on with their lives?

McCrumb does not want her ballad novels labeled as mysteries. How would you describe this novel to a friend?

See standard questions in the Introduction for more questions.

◇◇◀▬◆▬▶◇◇

Val McDermid

A Place of Execution

Val McDermid was born in 1955 in Kirkcaldy, Scotland. She received a B.A. in English from St. Hilda's College, Oxford, in 1975. From 1975 to 1991 she worked as a journalist in Devon and Manchester, England, as well as Glasgow, Scotland, before becoming a full-time writer. Her first novel, *Report for Murder*, was published in 1987 and featured reporter Lindsay Gordon. Other novels in this series include *Common Murder* (1989), *Final Edition* (1991), *Union Jack* (1993), *Booked for Murder* (1996), and *Hostage to Murder* (2003). Her series about P.I. Kate Brannigan includes *Dead Beat* (1992), *Kick Back* (1993), *Crackdown* (1994), *Clean Break* (1995), *Blue Genes* (1996), and *Star Struck* (1998). Her series about clinical psychologist Dr. Tony Hill and Detective Chief Inspector Carol Jordan includes *The Mermaids Singing* (1995—Gold Dagger Award from the Crime Writers' Association and the French Grand Prix des Romans d'Aventure for Mauvais Signes), *The Wire in the Blood* (1997), *The Last Temptation* (2002), and *The Torment of Others* (2004). In addition to *A Place of Execution*, she has written two other stand-alone novels, *Killing the Shadows* (2000) and *The Distant Echo* (2003—Barry Award for the Best British Crime Novel and the Sherlock Award), and two collections of short stories, *The Writing on the Wall* (1997) and *Stranded* (2005), and a nonfiction work on the fictional female P.I., called *A Suitable Job for a Woman* (1994).

Plot summary: George Bennett is willing to bare his soul to journalist Catherine Heathcote. The subject is the disappearance of thirteen-year-old Alison Carter from the gated community of Scardale in Derbyshire in 1963. This was Detective Inspector Bennett's first case. What has always haunted Bennett was his inability to piece together the puzzle that included no corpse and a closed community. Then, thirty years later, just before the publication of his story, Bennett withdraws from the interview, hiding new evidence that will reveal the truth. The dogged journalist is not about to give up that easily, and as Carter struggles to go over the ground Bennett has covered years earlier, she finds the community is still a closed book to outsiders.

Web site:
http://www.valmcdermid.com
Reader's guide:
none

Publication date: 2000

Number of pages: 403

Geographic setting: England, Derbyshire, Burxon; England, Derbyshire, Scardale

Time period: 1960s, 1990s

Series notes: This is a stand-alone novel.

Subject heading: Children at risk

Readalikes

Reginald Hill's *On Beulah Height*—similar use of plot

Andrew Pyper's *Lost Girls*—similar use of plot

Minette Walters—similar use of psychological suspense

Appeal points: This novel was a nominee for the Macallan Dagger and the Edgar Allan Poe award and won the Anthony, Barry, Dilys, and Macavity awards for best mystery novel of the year. It was chosen as a New York Times Notable Book of the Year and the Book of the Year citation from Los Angeles Times. This psychological thriller is a classic page-turner. Readers who are willing to be fooled should enjoy the experience.

DISCUSSION QUESTIONS

Why would McDermid choose a gated community for her setting?

Why does the gated community not protect these people from their tragedy?

Why do so many people work to obstruct the jobs of the police? Why will Ma Lomas not help Bennett on day two of the investigation?

This was George Bennett's first case. How did he do?

Why does the author have Bennett get physically ill twice in the story?

Who killed the other missing children?

Does the law work to protect the guilty, or the innocent?

How do you see the difference between the law and the administration of justice?

If you had been on the jury—what would you have decided?

When is vigilantism justified?

See standard questions in the Introduction for more questions.

◇◇◆◇◇

Maan Meyers

The Dutchman

Annette Brafman was born in 1934 in New York City. She earned a B.A. from Douglass College in 1955. From 1955 until 1960 she was a high school English teacher. Then Annette became the personal assistant to legendary Broadway producer Harold Prince; she worked for him from 1960 until 1976. She married Martin Meyers in 1963. Her mystery series featuring executive recruiters Smith and Wetson includes *The Big Killing* (1989), *Tender Death* (1990), *The Deadliest Option* (1991), *Blood on the Street* (1992), *Murder: The Musical* (1993), *These Bones Were Made for Dancin'* (1995), *The Groaning Board* (1997), and *Hedging* (2005). Her Olivia Brown series includes *Free Love* (1999) and *Murder Me Now* (2001). Her stand-alone novel is *Repentances* (2004).

Martin Meyers was born in 1934 in New York City, the son of a waiter and a cook. He attended the New York High School for the Performing Arts before serving in the Army from 1953 until 1955. He has appeared as an actor in numerous Broadway shows including "Zorba," as well as in film and television productions. His mystery series featuring private eye Patrick Hardy includes *Kiss and Kill* (1975), *Hung Up to Die* (1976), *Red Is for Murder* (1976), *Reunion for Death* (1976), and *Spy and Die* (1976). His stand-alone novels are *A Federal Case* (1978) and *Suspect* (1987).

Maan Meyers is the pseudonym of the husband and wife writing team of Annette and Martin Meyers. They live in New York City.

Plot summary: Pieter Tonneman is Schout (Sheriff) of New Amsterdam in 1664. He is a bit thick and mostly drunk, but when his friend is murdered, he rises to the occasion by launching an investigation. The bigger threat to the whole community is the impending invasion by the British. Racing against the inevitable fate of this colony, Tonneman searches for the killer.

Web site:
http://www.meyersmysteries.com
Reader's guide:
none

Publication date: 1992

Number of pages: 306

Geographic setting: New York, Manhattan (New Amsterdam Colony)

Time period: 1660s

Series notes: The Dutchman series actually relates the history of the Tonneman family over 200 years. This is the first novel, and the additional stories are told in *The Kingsbridge Plot* (1993), *The High Constable* (1994), *The Dutchman's Dilemma* (1995), *The House on Mulberry Street* (1996), and *The Lucifer Contract* (1997).

Readalikes

Barbara Hambly's Benjamin January series—similar use of character in a historical setting

Margaret K. Lawrence's Hannah Trevor series—similar use of character in a historical setting

Matthew Pearl's *The Dante Club*—similar use of character in a historical setting

Subject headings: Colonial America; Dutch colonies; New Amsterdam Colony

Appeal points: This novel should appeal to all lovers of historical mysteries.

DISCUSSION QUESTIONS

How did the authors create the historical atmosphere for this novel? What details do you remember?

What role does alcohol play in this novel?

How heroic is Pieter Tonneman?

Is it fair to judge Pieter?

What qualifications were required to be Schout?

Does Pieter rise to the occasion?

See standard questions in the Introduction for more questions.

◇◇◆◇◇

Denise Mina

Garnethill

Denise Mina was born in 1966 in Glasgow, Scotland, the daughter of an oil engineer. She received a law degree from Glasgow University and has studied in a Ph.D. program concentrating on mental illness in female crime offenders. Having held jobs in a meat factory, as a hospital nurse, and as a university tutor, Mina is now a full-time writer. She received the Macallan Short Story Dagger from the Crime Writers' Association for her short story "Helena and the Babies." Besides her novels about Maureen O'Donnell, she has written two stand-alone novels, *Sanctum* (2002) and *The Field of Blood* (2005). She lives in Glasgow.

Plot summary: Maureen O'Donnell has been out of the Northern Psychiatric Hospital in Glasgow for about six months. Trying to get her life together, she has decided to quit the affair she is having with the married psychologist Douglas Brady, a man she met at the sexual-abuse clinic. After a binge, she discovers Douglas tied to a kitchen chair in her living room, his throat slashed. Has she suppressed the memory of this murder? Maureen is the chief suspect of Detective Chief Inspector Joe McEwan. Forced to play the role of detective, Maureen begins to tie in rumors of inappropriate behavior and sexual abuse by the clinic's staff as she struggles to get her life together and prove herself innocent.

> **Web site:**
> none
> **Reader's guide:**
> none

Publication date: 1998

Number of pages: 348

Geographic setting: Scotland, Glasgow

Time period: 1990s

Series notes: This is the first book in a trilogy that includes *Exile* (2000) and *Resolution* (2001).

Subject headings: Mental illness; Sexual abuse

Appeal points: *Garnethill* won the John Creasey Memorial Dagger for best first crime novel from the Crime Writers' Association. This novel has a female voice that often appeals to readers looking for a flawed but determined heroine. The situations revealed in this novel are contemporary issues for the character and are very different from the concerns of Miss Marple. The gritty setting will appeal to readers who enjoy urban nightmare stories.

> **Readalikes**
> Ken Bruen's Jack Taylor series—similar use of character
> Vicki Hendricks—similar use of character

DISCUSSION QUESTIONS

Do you enjoy books set in foreign cultures?

What differences did you notice between Glasgow, Scotland, and most American cities?

How hard was this book to read because of the use of Scottish slang?

Do you prefer a book with a police detective or an amateur?

Is Maureen too much of an amateur?

What were the reasons Maureen has for starting an investigation?

What reasons did Maureen have for continuing the investigation?

When McEwan asks her to stop (p. 253), why does Maureen continue?

Is Maureen responsible for Martin Donegan's death?

Why is D. C. McAskil so nice to Maureen?

Which is worse, Michael's abuse or Winnie's denial?

Is Maureen an alcoholic?

How did you feel about Liam's drug dealing?

On page 247, Maureen asks, "But if we use violence, how are we different from them?"

Did you find this book funny? Can you mention any particular examples?

Is there any sense of hope in this book?

See standard questions in the Introduction for more questions.

◇◇◆◇◇

Walter Mosley

Devil in a Blue Dress

Walter Mosley was born in 1952 in Los Angeles, California, to a white Jewish mother who worked for the Los Angeles Department of Education and an African American father who worked as a custodian. Mosley attended Goddard College and then received a B.A. from Johnson State College in 1977. He worked as a computer programmer from 1982 until the publication of his first book. He earned an M.A. from the City University of New York in 1991. He married Joy Kellman, a dancer and choreographer, but they divorced in 2001. His first novel, *Gone Fishin'*, which introduces the character of Easy Rawlins as a young man, went unpublished until 1997. *Devil in a Blue Dress* is his first published novel, and begins Easy's stories. Mosley's other works are *R. L.'s Dream* (1995), *Always Outnumbered, Always Outgunned: The Socrates Fortlow Stories* (1998), *Blue Light* (1998), *Walkin' the Dog* (1999), *Workin' on the Chain Gang: Contemplating Our Chains at the End of the Millennium* (1999), *Fearless Jones* (2001), *Futureland: Nine Stories of an Imminent World* (2001), *What Next: A Memoir toward World Peace* (2003), *Fear Itself: A Mystery* (2003), *The Man in My Basement* (2004), and *47* (2005).

Plot summary: When Easy Rawlins is fired from his day job in 1948, he is desperate enough to accept a job from a white man. Dewitt Albright wants Easy to look for a woman in a blue dress. Things get complicated when it appears Daphne Monet is in the company of a gangster and in possession of someone else's money.

> **Web site:**
> http://www.twbookmark.com/features/
> waltermosley/index.html
> **Reader's guide:**
> none

Publication date: 1990

Number of pages: 219

Geographic setting: California, Los Angeles

Time period: 1940s

Series notes: This is the first book in the Easy Rawlins series. The rest are *A Red Death* (1991), *White Butterfly* (1992), *Black Betty* (1994), *A Little Yellow Dog* (1996), *Gone Fishin'* (1997—the first Rawlins story), *Bad Boy Brawly Brown* (2002—Hammett Prize nominee), *Six Easy Pieces: Easy Rawlins Stories* (2003), *Little Scarlet* (2004), and *Cinnamon* (2005).

Subject heading: African Americans

Appeal points: This novel was nominated for an Edgar and won the Shamus as the best first novel of the year. It will work in a novel-into-film discussion. Easy is a fascinating character who should appeal to all readers as a hero, but the combination with Mouse makes some readers flinch. This novel also wins over historical novel readers.

> **Readalikes**
> Kris Nelscott's Smokey Dalton series—similar use of character in a historical setting
> Gary Phillips' Ivan Monk series—similar use of character

DISCUSSION QUESTIONS

Why is Easy's home so important to him?

What details provided by the author put you in this era?

How would you describe Easy's view of the way the world works?

Is it possible for Easy to disappear into this world or will he always be unable to hide?

Easy thinks money may make his life easier. How does money affect him in this book?

Does it help or hurt Easy to have a friend like Mouse?

How far is Easy from the "white" world?

How far into the "white" world can Easy tread?

Mosley says he writes in a "jazz language." What examples of that writing style can you identify?

See standard questions in the Introduction for more questions.

◇◇◆◇◇

Kris Nelscott

A Dangerous Road

Kris Nelscott is the pseudonym of Kristine Kathryn Rusch. She was born in 1960 in Oneonta, New York, to a math professor and a homemaker. Kris earned a B.A. from the University of Wisconsin in 1982. From 1978 until 1986 she worked as a freelance journalist; she operated a frame shop from 1981 until 1984. In 1985 she attended the Clarion Writers Workshop at Michigan State University. She was married once before her current marriage to writer Dean Wesley Smith. While working as a secretary in Eugene, Oregon, from 1986 to 1989, she and Smith founded Pulphouse Publishing. Her first novel, *The White Mists of Power*, launched in 1991 a prolific career in the science fiction, fantasy, and mystery field that has garnered her many awards. She has published under a number of pseudonyms. She lives in Lincoln City, Oregon.

Plot summary: It's 1968, and Memphis is coming unglued under the weight of a garbage strike that in two months will lead to the death of Martin Luther King. Smokey Dalton, a childhood friend of King, is approached by a white woman named Laura Hathaway because her mother's will has left a legacy to Smokey. Eight years prior, Smokey had wrestled with his conscience when he was the recipient of an anonymous $10,000 passed on to him by white lawyer Shelby Bowler. Smokey suspects that he now knows the source of the first legacy he accepted. What frightens Smokey the most is that he wonders if his connection to Laura could be a familial one.

Web site:
none
Reader's guide:
none

Publication date: 2000

Number of pages: 325

Geographic setting: Tennessee, Memphis

Time period: 1960s

Series notes: This is the first book in a series that includes *Smoke-filled Rooms* (2001), *Thin Walls* (2002), *Stone Cribs* (2004), and *War at Home* (2005).

Subject headings: African Americans; Race relations

Appeal points: *A Dangerous Road* was nominated for an Edgar Award as the best novel of the year. This complex ballet of past and present, poverty and wealth, black and white gives great strength to this novel, and thematically it ranks far above the average P.I. fare. Smokey is a complex character, stoic at times, contrasted with a passionate drive to define himself as a black man in America during the sixties. Truly a major achievement, this novel may rank as a classic in the genre.

Readalikes
Gar Anthony Haywood's Aaron Gunnar series—similar use of character
Walter Mosley's Easy Rawlins series—similar use of character in a historical setting

DISCUSSION QUESTIONS

How did the historical setting work for you?

Whose story is this? What is appealing about a complex novel like this?

How did the author do a credible job of creating Smokey, a black man, considering it was written by a white female?

How is this a woman's book?

How strong a female character is Laura?

Once Laura learns her birthright is false, how does she lose her identity?

Who is betrayed more by the Hathaways, Laura or Smokey?

Neither Smokey nor Laura know who their parents are—so who should feel worse?

Does Smokey make a bigger mistake by sleeping with a client or by sleeping with a white woman?

Can society accept mixed-race couples better today than it did in the 1960s?

How does Smokey have a healthy self-image?

What hope is there for boys like Jimmy and Joe?

See standard questions in the Introduction for more questions.

◇◇◆◇◇

Carol O'Connell

Mallory's Oracle

Carol O'Connell was born in 1947 in New York City. She earned a B.F.A. from Arizona State University. Before becoming a novelist, she worked as a proof-reader and a copyeditor.

Plot summary: Detective Louis Marko-witz's body is found next to one of the victims of a serial killer who stalks elderly women. His adopted daughter, Sergeant Kathleen Mallory, sets out on a mission to find his killer. The problem is that Mallory is a former feral child who, despite her rearing in the Markowitz home, is a borderline sociopath. Mallory is an outsider on the force, happier to be talking to her computer than to any human. Does she have what it takes to find a murderer?

> **Web site:**
> none
> **Reader's guide:**
> none

Publication date: 1994

Number of pages: 286

Geographic setting: New York, New York

Time period: 1990s

Series notes: This is the first book in a series that includes *The Man Who Cast Two Shadows* (1995), *Killing Critics* (1996), *Stone Angel* (1997), *Judas Child* (1998), *Shell Game* (1999), *Crime School* (2002), *Dead Famous* (2003), and *Winter House* (2004).

Subject headings: Elderly; Orphans; Serial killers

Appeal points: This novel was an Edgar Award nominee. Some books are unique just by the very nature of the back story, and this novel is one of them. Readers are generally either fascinated by the main character or repulsed by her lack of humanity. In a sense, some compo-nents of this novel mirror horror fiction.

> **Readalikes**
> Jeff Lindsay's Dexter Morgan series—similar use of a damaged hero as the lead character

DISCUSSION QUESTIONS

What did Helen and Louis see in Mallory that made them adopt the young girl?

What is missing from a person like Mallory that separates her from other children of her age?

Do any of Helen's lessons reach Mallory?

What are more valuable: ethical standards or survival skills?

Why can Mallory relate to computers but not to people?

Why can she be so stoic at the scene of Markowitz's murder?

Can Mallory distinguish between right and wrong?

Will Mallory ever love?

See standard questions in the Introduction for more questions.

◇◇◆◇◇

Joseph O'Connor

Star of the Sea

Joseph O'Connor was born in 1963 in Glenageary, Ireland. His mother died in an automobile accident in 1985. O'Connor's famous siblings are Sinead O'Connor, the singer, and Eimear, the painter. He also has two brothers. O'Connor earned a B.A. in English and modern American literature in 1984 and an M.A. in Anglo-Irish literature in 1986, all from University College in Dublin. While working as a full-time writer, critic, and playwright, he also earned an M.A. in screenwriting from the Northern School of Film and Television at the University of Leeds. O'Connor's first novel, *Cowboys & Indians*, was published in 1991. He lives in Dublin.

Plot summary: Sailing from Ireland in 1847, the *Star of the Sea* is attempting to leave behind all the difficulties of a country wracked by famine. On board is Lord David Merridith and his family, the targets of an assassin named Pius Mulvey. The Merridiths' nanny, Mary Duane, is Mulvey's former fiancée and the widow of Mulvey's dead brother. American journalist Grantley Dixon is traveling home, hoping to continue his affair with Lady Merridith, while providing the narrative in the form of his diaries about the voyage. On the storm-tossed seas, this mix of characters, all with different goals, is heading more for tragedy than a safe port.

> **Web site:**
> none
>
> **Reader's guide:**
> http://www.readinggroupguides.com/guides3/star_of_the_sea1.asp or http://www.harcourtbooks.com/bookcatalogs/bookpage.asp?isbn=0156029669&option=reading

Publication date: 2002
Number of pages: 386
Geographic setting: Atlantic Ocean voyage
Time period: 1840s
Series notes: This is a stand-alone novel.
Subject headings: Immigration; Ocean travel
Appeal points: *Star of the Sea* was short-listed for Irish Novel of the Year. Although a very literary effort, the novel is not above serving as a suspenseful thriller. The conflict among the characters is compelling. The narrative style, told in the form of a newspaperman's diaries and interviews, is unique. The nonlinear storyline may not appeal to all readers.

> **Readalikes**
>
> James Bradley's *Wrack*—similar literary style
>
> Ian McEwan—similar literary style
>
> Matthew Pearl's *The Dante Club*—similar use of historical setting

DISCUSSION QUESTIONS

How much of mankind's history can be explained by the statement, "Treat a man like a savage and he will become one"?

Whose story is *Star of the Sea*?

Who was the most sympathetic character for you, and why?

What historical details stuck with you long after reading this novel?

Is it justified that Mary Duane and David Merridith are separated by "a question of duty"?

In Chapter 8, why does David expend so much effort to lie to his sisters in his letter home?

Are the actions of the Hibernian Defenders justified?

What words would you use to describe Pius Mulvey?

What role does music play in the novel?

Which characters learned the most in this novel?

Who loves the most in this novel?

How can it be that in the wealthiest kingdom in the world, people in Ireland were starving?

See standard questions in the Introduction for more questions.

◇◇◆◇◇

Sara Paretsky

Bitter Medicine

Sara Paretsky was born in 1947 in Ames, Iowa, the daughter of a scientist and a librarian. She earned a B.A. from the University of Kansas in 1967. After visiting Chicago to do volunteer social work, she moved there. From 1971 until 1974 Paretsky worked as a publications manager for a research company. She then worked as a freelance business writer for three years. In 1976 Paretsky married Courtenay Wright; the couple has three sons. She earned an M.B.A. and a Ph.D. from the University of Chicago in 1977. From 1977 until 1986, she was an advertising manager for an insurance company. Since 1986, Paretsky has been a full-time writer. She helped found the organization Sisters in Crime and served as its first President from 1987 to 1988. Her only nonseries novel is *Ghost Country* (1998). In 2005, she received The Eye, the Lifetime Achievement Award, from the Private Eye Writers of America. She lives in Chicago, Illinois.

Plot summary: Chicago private eye V. I. Warshawski manages to get Consuelo Alvarado to a hospital when the sixteen-year-old goes into premature labor, but not soon enough to save her or her baby's life. Warshawski is grief stricken as Consuelo was the younger sister of her best friend Lottie's secretary. Later V. I. is shocked when Lottie's assistant, Dr. Malcom Tregiere, is brutally murdered. Could the indifferent father of the baby or his gang be taking revenge, or is there some other more sinister reason for Malcolm's death? When Lottie's clinic is attacked by an antiabortion group, V. I. has more on her hands then she can handle.

> **Web site:**
> http://www.Paretskyparetsky.com
> **Reader's guide:**
> none

Publication date: 1987

Number of pages: 321

Geographic setting: Illinois, Chicago

Time period: 1980s

Series notes: Besides this novel, her Warshawski series includes *Indemnity Only* (1982), *Deadlock* (1984), *Killing Orders* (1985), *Blood Shot* (1988; also *Toxic Shock*—Silver Dagger Award winner), *Burn Marks* (1990), *Guardian Angel* (1992), *Tunnel Vision* (1994), *Windy City Blues* (1995), *Hard Time* (1999), *Total Recall* (2001), *Blacklist* (2003), and *Fire Sale* (2005).

> **Readalikes**
> Barbara D'Amato's Cat Marsala series—similar use of character and setting

Subject headings: Abortion; Gangs; Hospitals; Medical malpractice

Appeal points: This novel appeals to readers who are interested in a tough, urban tale. It looks at social issues as a major plot device as well as an underlying theme. Although tinged with a feminist perspective, that aspect of Paretsky's writing is what makes V. I. one of the most popular fictional characters in the private detective field today.

DISCUSSION QUESTIONS

What are the differences between V. I. and the classic male private eye?

Is V. I. too emotionally vulnerable to survive in the streets?

What kind of friend is V. I. Warshawski?

How should people like Consuelo receive medical care in America?

How evil is Fabiano Hernandez?

V. I. refers to gangs as "a cholera epidemic." How should we deal with this social, political, and sometimes criminal networking in our society?

What is the proper way to protest on an issue like abortion?

Who is responsible for the death of Peter Burgoyne?

Would you hire V. I. to be your detective?

See standard questions in the Introduction for more questions.

◇◇◆◇◇

Matthew Pearl

The Dante Club

Matthew Pearl was born in 1975 in New York. He has a B.A. in English and American literature from Harvard University and graduated in 2000 from the Yale Law School. Pearl has been a teaching fellow in literature at Harvard University and currently is an adjunct professor at Emerson College. He is an editor and provided the introduction to a translation of *Inferno* by Dante Alighieri published in 2003. Pearl received the Dante Prize from the Dante Society of America in 1998 for his senior thesis on the Dante Club. He lives in Cambridge, Massachusetts.

Plot summary: In Boston in 1865, a distinguished group of Americans including Henry Wadsworth Longfellow, James Russell Lowell, J. T. Fields, and Oliver Wendell Holmes, Sr., form the Dante Club to arrange for the publication of the first American translation of Dante's *Divine Comedy* from its original Italian. When people start dying based on the methods described in the *Inferno*, it is only these men who see the clues for what they are: someone desperately wants to prevent the publication of this book.

> **Web site:**
> http://www.thedanteclub.com
>
> **Reader's guide:**
> http://www.thedanteclub.com/
> bookclub.html

Publication date: 2003

Number of pages: 372

Geographic setting: Massachusetts, Boston

Time period: 1860s

Series notes: This is a stand-alone novel.

Subject headings: Dante Alighieri; Holmes, Oliver Wendell, Sr., Longfellow, Henry Wadsworth; Lowell, James Russell

Appeal points: This is a well-written and literary effort. Besides the book's obvious strength as a historical novel, Pearl manages to show the reader the great men of Boston and the common man in the same story. This novel works as a thriller as well.

> **Readalikes**
>
> Margaret Atwood's *The Blind Assassin*—similar literary style
>
> Dan Brown's *The Da Vinci Code*—similar plot, suspense, and thriller style
>
> Caleb Carr—similar historical plot
>
> Umberto Eco's *The Name of the Rose*—similar historical plot and style
>
> Anne Perry—similar use of historical setting

DISCUSSION QUESTIONS

What is the purpose of the preface?

Why would the men of the Dante Club risk all to have an American translation of Dante?

Can you think of any modern equivalent to the Dante Club?

Defend the Dante Club's decision to keep the cause of the violence in Boston to themselves?

Why does Holmes state "after a man begins to attack Boston . . . there is not much left of him"? (pp. 170–171).

What images of Boston do you get from this book?

How good are the Dante Club's members as detectives?

What is the meaning of Lowell's confession, "I forgot that I was a professor and felt as if I were something real"? (p. 251)

What is the meaning of Webster's confession on page 249?

What purpose does Patrolman Nicholas Rey serve in the book?

How much of the consequences of The Dante Club can be blamed on the cult of personality surrounding Longfellow?

After the death of his wife, Longfellow goes into hiding. What do you think he saw in Dante that gave him solace?

Loyalty is displayed numerous times in this book. Could we expect that same loyalty today from our friends and neighbors?

What is it that keeps Holmes from communicating with his son Wendy?

The Civil War has just ended in America. What images of postconflict America do you get from this book?

What is meant by the image of Teal chewing on and spitting out letters from books?

Do the victims of Teal deserve their fate?

What does the Protestant hierarchy of Boston have to fear from Catholicism and the immigrant class?

Many attempts are made to ban parts of culture (books, photographs, films, art, etc.). Can items of culture really cause bad things to happen?

See standard questions in the Introduction for more questions.

◇◇◆◇◇

Ellis Peters

The Virgin in the Ice

Edith Mary Pargeter was born in 1913 in Horsehay, Shropshire, England. From 1933 until 1940, she worked as a pharmacist's assistant in Dawley. During World War II, she served in the Women's Royal Naval Service, where she reached the rank of petty officer. Her first book, *Hortensius, Friend of Nero*, was published under her own name in 1936. Since then, she has published numerous historical, romantic, and contemporary novels. Pargeter's first mystery series, starring the Felse Family, began with *Fallen into the Pit* (1951), published under her own name. After this book, her novels were published under the pseudonym Ellis Peters. Her first Cadfael novel, *A Morbid Taste for Bones*, was published in 1977. She has also written novels under the pseudonyms Peter Benedict, Jolyon Carr, and John Redfern. She won an Edgar Award for *Death and the Joyful Woman* (1961). The author died in 1995.

Web site:
none
Reader's guide:
none

Plot summary: Brother Cadfael, of the Benedictine abbey of Saint Peter and Saint Paul, at Shrewsbury, is a former campaigner in the Crusades. Now he is an herbalist who likes to solve mysteries, and this novel is the sixth book in this series. In 1189, after the city of Worcester has been sacked during a civil war, two orphans from a noble family and a young nun have fled toward Shrewsbury seeking sanctuary, only to go missing. Then a woman's body is found frozen in a pond during the cold winter months, while a monk is found beaten and suffering from amnesia. It takes unusual strength of character on the part of the good Brother to solve this case.

Publication date: 1982
Number of pages: 202
Geographic setting: England, Shropshire, Shrewsbury
Time period: 1130s
Series notes: This series begins with *A Morbid Taste for Bones* (1977), *One Corpse Too Many* (1979), *Monk's-Hood* (1980), *Saint Peter's Fair* (1981), and *The Leper of St. Giles* (1981). After this novel, the series picks up with *The Sanctuary Sparrow* (1983), *The Devil's Novice* (1983), *Dead Man's Ransom* (1984), *The Pilgrim of Hate* (1984), *An Excellent Mystery* (1985), *The Raven in the Foregate* (1986), *The Rose Rent* (1987), *The Hermit of Eyton Forest* (1987), *The Confession of Brother Haluin* (1988), *A Rare Benedictine* (1988), *The Heretic's Apprentice* (1989), *The Potter's Field* (1990), *The Summer of the Danes* (1991), and *The Holy Thief* (1992).

Readalikes
Susan Witting Albert's China Bayles series—similar use of plot
Kathy Lynn Emerson's Susanna, Lady Appleton, series—similar use of plot
Sharan Newman's Catherine LeVendeur series—similar use of historical setting

Subject headings: Herbs; Monks

Appeal points: This novel was filmed for PBS and would work in a novel-into-film discussion. The gentle protagonist of this novel is a surprisingly good detective and he appeals to many readers. The historical details provided by the author make this one of the great historical mystery series of all times.

DISCUSSION QUESTIONS

How does the author use the landscape and the weather to set a mood?

Cadfael says he "chose this discipline for his cure." Is it working?

Why are Hugh and Brother Cadfael friends?

Who should feel guiltier: Yves or Elyas?

What meaning does the relationship between Olivier de Bretagne and Brother Cadfael mean?

Why does the author make a distinction between the way Hugh can celebrate being a father and the way that Brother Cadfael must?

See standard questions in the Introduction for more questions.

◇◇◆◇◇

Andrew Pyper

Lost Girls

Andrew Pyper was born in Stratford, Ontario, Canada, in 1968. He received a B.A. from McGill University and then a law degree from the University of Toronto. His collection of short stories, *Kiss Me*, was published in 1996. His other novels are *The Trade Mission* (2003; also: *Dark Descent*) and *The Wildfire Season* (2005). He lives in Toronto.

Plot summary: A pompous and drug-addicted Toronto attorney, Bartholomew Crane, heads north to Murdoch, Ontario, Canada, where two missing teenagers are believed drowned in the murky waters of Lake St. Christopher. Their high school English teacher, Thomas Tripp, is accused of murder, and Crane is assigned to defend the man. But what passes for reality in this gothic setting, especially when Crane is not in control of his own senses, presses the boundaries between reality and hallucination before the truth is revealed about what happened on that eerie lake.

> **Web site:**
> http://andrewpyper.com
> **Reader's guide:**
> none

Publication date: 1999

Number of pages: 388

Geographic setting: Canada, Ontario, Murdoch, Lake St. Christopher

Time period: 1990s

Series notes: This is a stand-alone novel.

Subject headings: Children at risk; Courtroom dramas; Drugs

Appeal points: This novel won the Arthur Ellis Award for best first mystery and received recognition from the Canadian Booksellers' Association, the Globe and Mail, the New York Times and London Evening Standard as one of the best mysteries of the year. This book has no hero, so it may be a tough sell to some readers. Its very dark setting may remind some readers of horror fiction rather than mystery. It also extensively uses magical realism.

> **Readalikes**
>
> Margaret Atwood's *The Blind Assassin*—similar literary style
>
> Thomas H. Cook's *The Chatham School Affair*—similar plot
>
> Henry James' *The Turn of the Screw*—similar literary style

DISCUSSION QUESTIONS

Are there other literary works or authors this work reminds you of?

Pyper says to qualify as a literary novel, a book must contain narrative voice, careful prose, and themes that extend beyond what happens next. How does this novel accomplish those goals?

Pyper says his novel explores his avowed obsessions that are fantasy vs. reality, the power of local mythology, and the phenomenon of disappearance. How does he accomplish these explorations?

Pyper says, "the standard psychological and sociological explanations of why certain men do this are inadequate, so I had to bring in the uncanny to explain the inexplicable." How did the book's use of these techniques appeal to you?

Was it hard to enjoy a novel without a heroic main character?

Who is the better lawyer—Barth Crane or Pete Goodwin? Why?

Do Barth's methods make him a bad lawyer or a bad person?

Who is the better father: Lloyd McConnell or Brian Flynn? Why?

Who would you want for a neighbor if you lived in Murdoch?

In chapter 42, Laird Johanssen says he "could" have been the murderer. Do we believe that everyone has the potential to be a murderer? If not, do we enjoy vicariously experiencing chaos in society, or as Barth says, "People have the right to be occasionally horrified"?

Who is the young stripper in the Empire Hotel? Who are the girls on the corner that Barth sees from his hotel window? Whose hair does Barth grab when he almost drowns?

Does the town of Murdoch have the right to pass judgment on The Lady in the Lake?

Did you find anything humorous in this novel?

React to these quotes:

> page 21—"There are no such things as lies . . . there are only mis-perceptions."
>
> page 13—"There is nothing more overrated in the practice of criminal law than the truth . . . the subtle distinction between the truth and the convincing of others to accept one of its alternatives."
>
> page 128—"What's far more amazing than how easily one can come to do wrongful things is the ease with which one can then go on to forget about them."
>
> page 191—"And this is the only really startling thing about the evil of the world: not that so much of it exists, but that nobody ever expects it."

See standard questions in the Introduction for more questions.

◇◇━◆━◇◇

Ellery Queen

Calamity Town

Ellery Queen is the pseudonym of two cousins, Frederic Dannay and Manfred Lee. In 1929, they entered and won a contest for their joint novel, but the contest's promise of publication fell through. However, the novel, *The Roman Hat Mystery*, was eventually published by Stokes in 1929. This novel launched the fictional detective career of the character Ellery Queen. It also launched one of the most successful careers in the mystery fiction field for its two authors, who chose to hide behind the same pseudonym as their character. Besides their literary output (including novels under the name Barnaby Ross), they established *Ellery Queen's Mystery Magazine* and the organization the Mystery Writers of America. They won an Edgar Award in 1945 for best radio program, in 1949 for their contribution to the field of the mystery short story, and were made Grand Masters in 1960. Dannay was born Daniel Nathan in 1905 in Brooklyn, New York. He married three times and is the father of two sons. He worked in the advertising industry before becoming a full-time writer. He died in 1982. Lee was born Manford Lepofsky in 1905 in Brooklyn, New York. In 1925 he earned a B.S. from New York University. Before becoming a full-time writer, he worked for motion picture companies as a publicity and advertising man. He married Catherine Brinker; they had eight children. He died in 1971.

Web site:
none
Reader's guide:
none

Plot summary: Detective Ellery Queen needs to escape to a quiet place to write his next novel, and his choice is Wrightsville. Stepping off the train in the guise of Ellery Smith, he just wants to be left alone. But when he decides to lease "Calamity House" from the Wright family, it drags him into their life. Newlyweds Jim Haight and Nora Wright find themselves wondering about the cause when she falls ill soon after the arrival of Jim's sister Rosemary. But on New Year's Eve it is Rosemary who is found dead from arsenic poisoning, and the visiting detective is called in to discover who did it.

Publication date: 1942
Number of pages: 318
Geographic setting: New York, Wrightsville
Time period: 1940s
Series notes: This is the fifteenth novel in the series. The other titles are *The Roman Hat Mystery* (1929), *The French Powder Mystery* (1930), *The Dutch Shoe Mystery* (1931), *The Greek Coffin Mystery* (1932), *The Egyptian Cross Mystery* (1932), *The American Gun Mystery* (1933), *The Siamese Twin Mystery* (1933), *The Chinese Orange Mystery* (1934), *The Spanish Cape Mystery* (1935), *Halfway House* (1936), *The Door Between* (1937), *The Devil to Pay* (1938), *The Four of Hearts* (1938), *The Dragon's Teeth* (1939), *There Was an Old Woman* (1943),

The Murderer Is a Fox (1945), *Ten Days' Wonder* (1948), *Cat of Many Tails* (1949), *Double, Double* (1950), *The Origin of Evil* (1951), *The King Is Dead* (1952), *The Scarlet Letters* (1953), *Inspector Queen's Own Case* (1956), *The Finishing Stroke* (1958), *The Player on the Other Side* (1963—ghostwritten by Theodore Sturgeon), *And on the Eighth Day* (1964—ghostwritten by Avram Davidson), *The Fourth Side of the Triangle* (1965—ghostwritten by Avram Davidson), *A Study in Terror* (1966—ghostwritten by Paul W. Fairman), *Face to Face* (1967), *The House of Brass* (1968—ghostwritten by Avram Davidson), *The Last Woman in His Life* (1970), and *A Fine and Private Place* (1971).

Subject headings: Authors; Poisons; Rural towns

Appeal points: As one of the leading proponents of the puzzle novel that defined the Golden Age of mysteries, these authors will always deliver a "play fair" mystery. This novel makes a breakthrough in this series as the Queen character becomes more believable while the novels begin to deal with "why" as much as "who."

> **Readalikes**
>
> Agatha Christie's Jane Marple series—similar style and use of character

DISCUSSION QUESTIONS

How good a job did the authors do of presenting a small-town environment?

How easy was it for Ellery to operate under an alias? Would it be that easy today?

How would you describe Patricia? How is she different from Nora? Is the portrait of Lola accurate for its time? How have women's roles changed regarding marriage and divorce?

Did you enjoy the romances that are displayed in this book?

How have courtroom scenes changed since this novel was written?

See standard questions in the Introduction for more questions.

◇◇◆◇◇

Ian Rankin

Black and Blue

Ian Rankin was born in 1960 in Cardenden, Fife, Scotland. Rankin earned an M.A. from the University of Edinburgh in 1982. He worked variously as a taxman, hi-fi journalist, musician, and at other odd jobs before becoming a full-time writer. His first novel, *The Flood,* was published in 1986. Additional nonseries novels include *Watchman* (1988) and *Westwind* (1990). His first Rebus novel, *Knots & Crosses*, was published in 1987. Under the pseudonym Jack Harvey he has written *Witch Hunt* (1993), *Bleeding Hearts* (1994), and *Blood-Hunt* (1995). *Beggars Banquet* (2002) is a collection of non-Rebus short stories. His awards include the Dagger Award for best short story of 1994. He is married, has two sons, and lives in Edinburgh.

Plot summary: The serial killer "Bible John" worked the Glasgow area in the 1960s, becoming a criminal legend. Now, someone is copying his style and starting a new killing spree. Rebus, however, is assigned the murder case of oilman Allan Mitchison, who died in a suburb of Edinburgh. But when Rebus' investigation takes him north to the oil rigs located off the coast at Aberdeen, he finds his case is linked to the media's new darling, copycat serial killer "Johnny Bible."

> **Web site:**
> http://www.ianrankin.net
> **Reader's guide:**
> *Ian Rankin's Black and Blue: A Reader's Guide* by Gill Plain (Continuum, 2002).

Publication date: 1997

Number of pages: 393

Geographic setting: Scotland, Aberdeen; Scotland, Edinburgh; Scotland, North Sea

Time period: 1990s

Series notes: The Rebus series begins with *Knots and Crosses* (1987), *Hide and Seek* (1991), *Tooth and Nail* (1992—also: *Wolfman*), *A Good Hanging and Other Stories* (1992), *Strip Jack* (1992), *The Black Book* (1993), *Mortal Causes* (1994), and *Let It Bleed* (1995). After *Black and Blue* (the eighth novel), the series continues with *The Hanging Garden* (1998), *Death Is Not the End* (1998), *Dead Souls* (1999—Dagger Award nominee), *Set in Darkness* (2000), *The Falls* (2001), *Resurrection Men* (2002—Edgar Award winner), *A Question of Blood* (2003), and *Fleshmarket Close* (2004).

Subject headings: Oil; Serial killers

Appeal points: This novel was nominated for an Edgar and won the Gold Dagger as the best mystery of the year. Sprawling across Scotland, this novel touches on many aspects of this country and should appeal to readers who are interested in journeying there. The dark

> **Readalikes**
>
> Ken Bruen's Jack Taylor series—similar use of character
>
> Michael Connelly's Harry Bosch series—similar use of character
>
> John Harvey's Charlie Resnick series—similar use of character

character of Rebus is explored here so the main character at times is portrayed almost with the same characteristics as the antihero.

DISCUSSION QUESTIONS

How can a society prevent money from corrupting its police force?

How guilty is John Rebus?

How obsessive is John Rebus?

How does alcohol affect this novel?

Does Allan Mitchison deserve his fate?

What role does Lenny Spaven play in the novel?

Why do we like to read about clever serial killers?

How does the author raise sympathy for Bible John?

See standard questions in the Introduction for more questions.

◇◇◆◇◇

Peter Robinson

In a Dry Season

Peter Robinson was born in 1950 in Castleford, Yorkshire, England, the son of a photographer and a homemaker. Robinson earned a B.A. in English literature from the University of Leeds in 1974. After moving to Canada he earned an M.A. from the University of Windsor in 1975, and a Ph.D. from York University in 1983. Since that time, Robinson has taught writing and literature classes. His non-Banks novel *Caedmon's Song* (U.S. title: *The First Cut*) was published in 1990. His short story "Innocence" won the CWC Award in 1991, and his story "The Two Ladies of Rose Cottage" was nominated for an Agatha and Ellis while winning the Macavity award. "Murder in Utopia" won the Ellis in the same year that "Missing In Action" won the Edgar for best short story. In 2002 Robinson was awarded the Dagger in the Library by the Crime Writers' Association. He is married to Shelia Halladay, a lawyer, and they live in Toronto, Canada.

Plot summary: Detective Chief Inspector Alan Banks is assigned the case when Thornfield Reservoir dries up and a skeleton is exposed, wrapped in World War II blackout curtains. Helped by his partner on the case, Detective Sergeant Annie Cabbot, he begins to probe into the history of Hobb's End. They discover the corpse is Gloria Shackleton, wife of World War II–vet Matthew Shackleton. Reaching back to World War II via the remembrances of Gwen, Matthew's sister, the novel bounces from past to present as it slowly begins to unveil the hidden secrets in this tragic village.

> **Web site:**
> http://www.inspectorbanks.com
> **Reader's guide:**
> none

Publication date: 1999

Number of pages: 422

Geographic setting: England, Yorkshire, Hobb's End

Time period: 1990s

Series notes: The Banks series of novels begins with *The Gallows View* (1987—nominated for the Creasey and Ellis awards), *A Dedicated Man* (1988—nominated for an Ellis Award), *A Necessary End* (1989), *The Hanging Valley* (1989—nominated for an Ellis Award), *Past Reason Hated* (1991—Ellis Award winner), *Wednesday's Child* (1992—Edgar Award nomination), *Final Account* (1994—also *Dry Bones That Dream*), *No Cure for Love* (1995), *Innocent Graves* (1996—Hammett Award nomination and an Ellis winner), *Blood at the Root* (1997), *Not Safe after Dark and Other Stories* (1998—contains three Banks stories). After *In a Dry Season*, the series continues with *Cold Is the*

> **Readalikes**
>
> Reginald Hill's *On Beulah Height*—similar use of plot
>
> J. Wallis Martin's *A Likeness in Stone*—similar use of plot
>
> Ian Rankin's John Rebus series—similar use of character

Grave (2000—an Ellis Award winner), *Aftermath* (2001), *The Summer That Never Was* (2003—U.S. title: *Close to Home;* nominated for an Anthony and an Ellis Award), *Playing with Fire* (2004), and *Strange Affair* (2005).

Subject headings: Reservoirs; Serial killers; World War II

Appeal points: This novel won the Anthony, Barry, France's Grand Prix de Litterature Policiere, and Sweden's Martin Beck Award. It was also nominated for the Edgar, Ellis, Hammett, and Macavity awards.

DISCUSSION QUESTIONS

What can Banks do about his relationship with Riddle?

How do Banks and Cabbot get along?

How does the author make the pastoral setting of Hobb's End into a crime scene?

How does the author use the past to create a sense of atmosphere surrounding Hobb's End?

How do the remembrances of Vivian Elmsley and the modern tale combine to tell this story?

What factors led to the concealment of the murder until the reservoir is drained?

What keeps Banks from being honest with his own son?

Did Frank Stringer deserve his fate?

Did Matthew deserve his fate?

See standard questions in the Introduction for more questions.

◇◇◆◇◇

S. J. Rozan

Shira J. Rozan was born in the Bronx, New York. She earned a B.A. from Oberlin College and an M.Arch. from the State University of New York at Buffalo. A former architect in a practice that focused on police stations, firehouses, and zoos, Rozan is now a full-time writer. She lives in lower Manhattan. Her short story "Hoops" was nominated for an Edgar Award, and her short story "Double-Crossing Delancy" was an Edgar Award winner.

> **Web site:**
> http://www.sjrozan.com

Absent Friends

Plot summary: In the days after September 11, a fund is set up in the memory of Jimmy McCaffery, a heroic New York City fireman who died in the towers. As a newspaperman named Harry Randall starts writing about Jimmy, he begins to unravel a story of deceit that involves Jimmy's childhood friends from Staten Island and possible payoffs to cover up a murder committed twenty years ago. When Randall jumps from a bridge, his lover and fellow reporter, Laura Stone, sets out to find the truth, believing that Harry would never have committed suicide. Before she is through, she has made several people reveal secrets that have been kept for years about a death they would all like to forget.

> **Reader's guide:**
> none

Publication date: 2004

Number of pages: 367

Geographic setting: New York, New York

Time period: 2000s

Series notes: This is a stand-alone novel.

Subject headings: Fire fighters; September 11, 2001; Terrorist attacks

Appeal points: Approaching a subject as painful as 9/11 is difficult for some readers. However, this novel focuses on the effect of the event on individuals and steers clear of the international politics that caused the event. This approach allows an examination of heroism without getting lost in the angst of the history.

> **Readalikes**
>
> Lawrence Block's *Small Town*—similar use of theme
>
> Earl W. Emerson—similar use of character
>
> Dennis Lehane's *Mystic River*—similar literary style
>
> Laura Lippman's *Every Secret Thing*—similar literary style

DISCUSSION QUESTIONS

Which detail about the city after the firestorm of 9/11 remains with you?

How did the author's style of using multiple points of view affect your reading of this book?

How did the author's style of shifting time enhance the storytelling?

Is it true that Jimmy never learned that sometimes you have to "let something go to save something else" (p. 5)?

What is the proper response when Marian asks Harry "only to help" and not to report what he has discovered about Jimmy?

Can Marian tell the difference between the Superman image and the real Jimmy?

Why won't Sally leave Pleasant Hills to marry Phil?

Why does Jimmy agree to Mike the Bear's request?

What would have happened if Jimmy would have delivered the news to Jack instead of Markie?

Why did Markie need to be Superman?

See standard questions in the Introduction for more questions.

◇◇◆◇◇

Winter and Night

Plot summary: Bill Smith, private investigator, is called out of bed one night to rescue his estranged sister Helen's son, Gary Russell, from the New York Police. When the young boy takes off after being rescued, Bill is forced to visit his sister in Warrenstown, New Jersey. There he discovers that a local obsession with high school football and the freedom this allows some of the players may have dramatic consequences for his nephew. Enlisting the help of his partner, Lydia Chin, from whom he has hidden the fact that he even has a sister, brings Bill's personal feelings to the forefront.

> **Reader's guide:**
> none.

Publication date: 2002
Number of pages: 338
Geographic setting: New Jersey, Warrenstown
Time period: 2000s
Series notes: This is the eighth book in this series. The other titles are *China Trade* (1994), *Concourse* (1995—Shamus Award winner), *Mandarin Plaid* (1996), *No Colder Place* (1997—Anthony and Shamus award nominations), *A Bitter Feast* (1998), *Stone Quarry* (1999), and *Reflecting the Sky* (2001—Edgar Award nomination and Shamus Award winner).
Subject headings: Family; Football
Appeal points: This novel won the Anthony and Edgar awards as the best novel of the year. Readers who are familiar with this series know that the point of

view of each book alternates between Lydia Chin and Bill Smith. The constant struggle to understand the relationship between Lydia and Bill appeals to readers. The inclusion of high school football in the plot may attract male readers.

Readalikes
Harlan Coben's Myron Bolitar series—similar use of sports
Eddie Muller's Billy Nichols series—similar use of sports
Jonathan Valin's *Life's Work*—similar use of sports

DISCUSSION QUESTIONS

Why do people like Bill fall away from their families? Is there any way he could have prevented the separation?

Why is Bill incapable of sharing his family history with his partner Lydia?

What does Warrenstown fail to give to a boy like Gary?

What role does Scott play in this novel? How does he fail as a father?

What role does Helen play in this novel? How does she fail as a mother?

What fails in the life of a boy like Paul?

What role should sports coaches play in the lives of young athletes? Is winning at all costs the best philosophy?

How much pressure should be placed on teenagers to perform in sports?

See standard questions in the Introduction for more questions.

Jamie M. Saul

Light of Day

Jamie M. Saul was born in New York City. He earned a B.A. from Indiana State University. He has been a scholarship student at Bread Loaf Writers' Conference, and his short fiction has been published in various magazines. He has served as a guest professor at Yale University.

Web site:
http://www.authortracker.ca/
author.asp?a=authorid&b=28341

Reader's guide:
none

Plot summary: Professor Jack Owens has fled New York for a small college campus in Indiana. He is shocked when he is told one day that his fifteen-year-old son Danny has committed suicide. Wallowing in his grief, he speculates on his role in the death of his son. Then, one day, he is visited by a police officer, who begins to open a door that Jack may not want to go through.

Publication date: 2005
Number of pages: 324
Geographic setting: Indiana, Gilbert
Time period: 2000s
Series notes: This is a stand-alone novel.
Subject headings: Academia; Children at risk; Suicide

Readalikes

Jacqueline Mitchard's *Deep End of the Ocean*—similar use of theme

---

Appeal points: Reading this painful novel about obsessive guilt is like poking a sharp stick in the reader's eye, and it does not appeal to those seeking a gentle read. It is an emotionally charged literary work that has a big payoff at the end.

DISCUSSION QUESTIONS

Does the author's style confirm "the blank parts suggest what's there as well as what's not there" (p. 156)?

What does the birth of Danny do to Jack and Anne's "Bohemian" life? What does this tell us about their characters?

What justifies Anne's actions?

Jack wonders (p. 67), "God sent her [Kim Connor] to Danny just to be five minutes late." Are we victims of fate, or is life and death this random?

How and why does Danny end up with Anne's orange button?

Why does Marty bond with Jack?

How bad a cop is Hopewell?

How guilty is the Cyberkiller?

How guilty should Jack feel?

What is more important, honesty or loyalty?

What does the book's conclusion mean to you?

See standard questions in the Introduction for more questions.

◇◇◆◇◇

Dorothy L. Sayers

Dorothy Leigh Sayers was born in 1893 in Oxford, England, the daughter of a clergyman and schoolmaster. Sayers was one of the first women to attend and graduate from Oxford, earning a B.A. in 1915 from Somerville College. She went on to earn an M.A. and B.C.L. in 1920. Sayers held a variety of teaching, publishing, and advertising jobs before becoming a full-time writer in 1931. She married Oswald Fleming in 1926, and they had one son. Sayers was one of the cofounders of the Detection Club. Besides her mystery writing, she was the author of Christian drama, essays, literary criticism, literary novels, poetry, radio plays, short stories, and translations. Sayers died in 1957 in Witham, Essex.

Series notes: Both of these novels reside in the Lord Peter Wimsey series. The titles featuring him are *Whose Body?* (1923), *Clouds of Witness* (1926), *Unnatural Death* (1927—U.S. title: *The Dawson Pedigree*), *The Unpleasantness at the Bellona Club* (1928), *Lord Peter Views the Body* (1928), *Strong Poison* (1930), *The Five Red Herrings* (1931—U.S. title: *Suspicious Characters*), *Have His Carcase* (1932), *Murder Must Advertise* (1933), *Hangman's Holiday* (1933), *The Nine Tailors* (1934), *Gaudy Night* (1935), *Busman's Honeymoon* (1937), *In the Teeth of the Evidence* (1939), and *Lord Peter* (1972).

> **Web site:**
> http://www.sayers.org.uk

Gaudy Night

> **Reader's guide:**
> none

Plot summary: Harriet Vane returns to Shrewsbury College, Oxford, for her "Gaudy," or class reunion. She gets to act as the detective when others of her graduating class begin to suffer personal attacks through poison-pen letters. While Lord Peter does arrive at the end to help, this novel is predominantly a look at the role of women in English society at this time, and how Harriet will handle the responsibility of solving the crimes.

Publication date: 1935

Number of pages: 469

Geographic setting: England, Oxford

Time period: 1930s

Subject headings: Academia; Class reunions

Appeal points: This novel steps away from Lord Peter and gives Harriet a chance to

> **Readalikes**
>
> Colin Dexter's Inspector Morse series—similar setting and use of character
>
> Veronica Stallwood's *Oxford Mourning*—similar use of setting

shine. It should appeal to readers who will not mind that there is no murder in this story.

DISCUSSION QUESTIONS

How important is higher education in the lives of these women?

Why does the college fail to take a more vigorous interest in the incidents?

How justified was the act of sending the poison-pen letters?

How much should anyone identify themselves with their work?

Can you identify what sets the classes apart in this novel?

What is Harriet's role in this novel? How does she function as the detective?

Sayers was considering setting Lord Peter aside and continuing with Harriet as the lead character. Why would you have like or disliked that decision?

How should Harriet deal with her feelings for Lord Peter?

In what ways could Harriet represent the feelings and opinions of the author?

How did the author maintain a mystery without using a murder? Did you miss it?

See standard questions in the Introduction for more questions.

◇◇◆◇◇

The Nine Tailors

Plot summary: In the East Anglia country, there is a church where the tolling of the bells is a religion unto itself. Stranded by a snowstorm, Lord Peter agrees to help Reverend Venables when one of his bellringers falls ill. Months later, when Lady Thorpe's death and burial reveal an additional body, Lord Peter is called in to devise an explanation.

Reader's guide:
none

Publication date: 1934
Number of pages: 311
Geographic setting: England, East Anglia, Fenchurch St. Paul
Time period: 1930s
Subject headings: Bells; Churches
Appeal points: This is a classic Golden Age mystery novel with all the conventions of the genre, so readers should bear that in mind. It is also an enlightened and literate affair, which

Readalikes
P. D. James' *Death in Holy Orders*—similar use of plot

appeals to readers who want to broaden their knowledge; it contains an enormous amount of bell-ringing information, which may not appeal to all readers.

DISCUSSION QUESTIONS

This is a classic Golden Age puzzle novel? How did the plot work for you? Were you able to guess the murderer's identity?

What did you learn about bell ringing?

What role does religious belief play in this novel?

How does this book distinguish between guilt and innocence?

How does this novel portray a rural village lifestyle? Was life ever this pastoral? Why must death intervene?

Sayers says that Reverend Thomas Venables was modeled on her father. How does the author treat this character and what does this tell us about her family life?

In this novel, sin brings its own punishment. What potential does anyone have to commit a murder?

See standard questions in the Introduction for more questions.

◇◇◆◇◇

Steven Saylor

Roman Blood

Steven Saylor was born in 1956 in Port Lavaca, Texas. In 1978 he earned a B.A. from the University of Texas. Saylor has been domestic partners with Richard K. Solomon since the 1970s. During the 1980s he worked as the fiction editor of *Drummer* magazine. In 1993 Saylor won the Robert L. Fish Memorial Award for best debut short story in the mystery genre for "A Will Is a Way." Under the pseudonym Aaron Travis, he has published *Big Shots* (1993), *Beast of Burden* (1993), and *Slaves of the Empire* (1996). His stand-alone novels include *A Twist at the End: A Novel of O. Henry* (2000) and *Have You Seen Dawn* (2003).

Plot summary: Cicero, a young lawyer in Rome, has taken over for Hortensius, a prominent defender, in the case of Sextus Roscius, accused of patricide. Seeking clues to Sextus' innocence, Cicero hires Gordianus the Finder to

> **Web site:**
> http://www.stevensaylor.com
> **Reader's guide:**
> none

seek the truth, and the investigation soon reveals that 80 B.C. is not an opportune time to seek law and order. With Sulla as its dictator, Rome has fallen into social disrepair, and the enemies of the emperor are being proscribed, their heads displayed at the Forum. On a journey to Roscius' homeland of Ameria, Gordianus becomes confused when he hears that the murdered father might have been proscribed despite being a Sulla supporter and despite the fact that political vendettas have been over for months. Roscius' cousins Magnus and Capito are gobbling up the dead man's property, while in Rome their conspiracy almost leads to Gordianus' death.

Publication date: 1991

Number of pages: 357

Geographic setting: Italy, Ancient Rome; Rome, Ancient; Umbria

Time period: 80s B.C.

Series notes: This is the first novel in the Roma Sub Rosa series featuring Gordianus the Finder. The rest of the series includes *Arms of Nemesis* (1992), *Catilina's Riddle* (1993), *The Venus Throw* (1995), *A Murder on the Appian Way* (1996), *The House of the Vestals* (1997), *Rubicon* (1998), *Last Seen in Massilia* (2000), *A Mist of Prophecies* (2002), *The Judgment of Caesar* (2004), and *A Gladiator Dies Only Once* (2005).

Subject headings: Ancient Rome; Cicero, Marcus Tullius; Gordian III; Patricide; Rome—History—Republic, 265–230 B.C.

Appeal points: This novel appeals to readers of historical novels. The mixture of politics and corruption appeals to modern readers.

> **Readalikes**
>
> Lindsey Davis' Didius Falco series—similar use of character in a historical setting
>
> John Maddox Roberts' SPQR series—similar use of character in a historical setting

DISCUSSION QUESTIONS

Did the author get the history right for you?

Did the politics of Ancient Rome remind you of our nation?

What is the role of Cicero in this novel?

How good a detective is Gordianus the Finder?

Is there a future for Gordianus and Bethesda?

What life was there for women like Elena?

How did you feel about the character of Tiro? What is the role of slavery in this novel?

See standard questions in the Introduction for more questions.

◇◇◆◇◇

Short Stories
Ernest Hemingway
"The Killers"
Cornell Woolrich
"Rear Window"

Ernest Hemingway was born in 1899 in Oak Park, Illinois, the son of a physician and a music teacher. While a professional writer most of his life, he had some experience as a reporter/correspondent and served as an ambulance driver for the Red Cross during World War I. His books include *The Torrents of Spring* (1926), *The Sun Also Rises* (1926), *A Farewell to Arms* (1929), *To Have and Have Not* (1937), *For Whom the Bell Tolls* (1940), *Across the River and into the Trees* (1950), *The Old Man and the Sea* (1952), *Islands in the Stream* (1970), and *The Garden of Eden* (1986), as well as numerous short-story collections and works of nonfiction.

> **Web site:**
> none
> **Reader's guide:**
> none

In 1953, he was awarded the Pulitzer Prize for *The Old Man and the Sea*, and he received the Nobel Prize for Literature. Hemingway married four times and had three children. He committed suicide in 1961.

Plot summary for "The Killers": Two men walk into Henry's lunch counter. They are not shy about telling the occupants, including Nick Adams, that they are there to kill the Swede, Ole Andreson. After tying up the occupants, they set about their task. Nick escapes to tell Ole of his fate and learn a valuable lesson about life.

Publication date: 1927
Number of pages: 8
Geographic setting: Illinois, Summit
Time period: 1920s
Series notes: This is the first of many stories Hemingway published about the character of Nick Adams collected in *The Nick Adams Stories* (1972).
Subject heading: Gangs

Cornell George Hopley-Woolrich was born in 1903 in New York City. Woolrich attended Columbia University from 1921 until 1925. A full-time writer from 1926 until his death, Woolrich wrote under his own name and under the pen names George Hopley and William Irish. He died in 1968.

Plot summary for "Rear Window": Confined to his bedroom with nothing better to do than stare out his window, Hal Jeffries becomes convinced that the neighbor he can see in

> **Readalikes**
> Raymond Chandler—similar use of dialog
> Dashiell Hammett—similar use of dialog

the flat across the way has murdered his wife. He uses his man, Sam, to do some legwork. Eventually, his probing draws the attention of the murderer, who may be making a decision to eliminate the only witness to his crime.

Publication date: 1942
Number of pages: 29
Geographic setting: Unknown
Time period: 1940s
Series notes: This is a stand-alone short story.

Subject headings: Photography; Voyeurism

Appeal points: The biggest appeal to members of your reading group for these short stories is that they are short. However, the form should not be dismissed because of their brevity. Hemingway's story is an early example of his quest to write about men and the code they live by. Its appeal is the abrupt and rapid style used to convey the plot to the reader and the crisp and believable dialog. Woolrich's story is a fine example of using pace in a brief space to create tension and suspense. Both of these short stories were made into films and work well in a film discussion session.

Readalikes

Edgar Allan Poe—similar use of theme

Josephine Tey's *The Daughter of Time*—similar use of plot

DISCUSSION QUESTIONS

How do Al and Max try to gain power over their victims?

How does Thorwald try to gain power over his victim?

What irony do you see in the fact that a "kosher" gunman calls Sam a "nigger" in "The Killers"?

What hints do we have that Sam in "Rear Window" is black?

Why does Max say George will make someone "a nice wife"?

Would Al and Max have killed the occupants of the lunchroom if the Swede had showed?

Why does Nick go to warn Ole but Sam stays out of it?

Why does Hal not leave things alone?

Why does Ole not want to escape his fate?

What are the different messages these authors give the reader about accepting fate?

See standard questions in the Introduction for more questions.

◇◇◆◇◇

Steven Sidor

Skin River

Steven Sidor was born in Chicago. He attended Grinnell College and the University of North Carolina at Chapel Hill. His short stories have appeared in a variety of print and on-line publications. His second novel, *Bone Factory*, was published in 2005. He lives with his wife and children near the Fox River in the greater Chicago area.

Plot summary: Buddy Bayes is hiding out in northern Wisconsin, running a small bar in a fishing and hunting haven, with designs of romancing his upstairs tenant, Margot. When an evil serial killer called the Goatskinner operates in this remote area, and Buddy just happens to be the search party member who finds a severed hand floating in the Skin River, it draws unwanted attention to him. The consequences of an old crime comes calling on him and Buddy finds himself caught between his past and the evil of the present.

Publication date: 2004

Number of pages: 241

Geographic setting: Wisconsin, Gunnar

Time period: 2000s

Series notes: This is a stand-alone novel.

Subject headings: Alcohol; Vengeance

Appeal points: This novel generally appeals to fans of the hard-boiled mystery. It makes great use of its remote setting.

Web site:
http://www.stevensidor.com

Reader's guide:
none

Readalikes

Lawrence Block's Matthew Scudder series—similar use of the effects of alcoholism

James Lee Burke—similar use of plot

DISCUSSION QUESTIONS

What sense of place does this novel provide?

Does a rural setting provide a retreat from crime, or is that an urban illusion?

What does the Skin River symbolize for the reader?

What is our fascination with serial killers?

Why do you think the author chose to use third person present in some sections of this book?

What role do parents play in this novel?

How should society deal with a person like "The Goatskinner"?

Why is Margot attracted to a person like Buddy?

Does Buddy deserve his fate?

Is there anything redeeming about the characters in this book?

See standard questions in the Introduction for more questions.

◇◇◆◇◇

Dana Stabenow

A Cold-Blooded Business

Dana Stabenow was born in 1952 in Anchorage, Alaska, and was raised on a seventy-five-foot fishing tender. In 1973 she earned a B.A. from the University of Alaska in journalism; she went on to earn an M.F.A. in 1985. Having held a variety of odd jobs (including egg grader and Alaska pipeline worker), Stabenow is now a full-time fiction writer. Her first novels were in the Star Svensdotter science fiction series, including *Second Star* (1991), *A Handful of Stars* (1991), and *Red Planet Run* (1995). Besides her Kate Shugak series, she has a mystery series featuring Alaskan State Trooper Liam Campbell and bush pilot Wyanet Chouinard, which includes *Fire and Ice* (1998), *So Sure of Death* (1999), and *Nothing Gold Can Stay* (2000).

Plot summary: Kate Shugak gets hired as a roustabout in Prudhoe Bay so that she can discover who is bringing coke into RPetCo's territory. The big oil company is nervous enough having just suffered a big spill and does not need or want a scandal. Kate learns that the oil company is made up of people whom she can really care for and surprisingly, she can even admit that environmentally the company is doing all they can. Her anger rises when she discovers someone may be smuggling ancient native artifacts off the Slope, and her investigation of this leads to the solution of the drug problem.

> **Web site:**
> http://www.stabenow.com
> **Reader's guide:**
> none

Publication date: 1994

Number of pages: 231

Geographic setting: Alaska, North Slope; Alaska, Prudhoe Bay

Time period: 1990s

Series notes: This is the fourth novel in the Kate Shugak series, which began with *A Cold Day for Murder* (1992—Edgar Award for best paperback original), *A Fatal Thaw* (1993), and *Dead in the Water* (1993). After *A Cold-Blooded Business*, she wrote *Play with Fire* (1995), *Blood Will Tell* (1996), *Breakup* (1997), *Killing Grounds* (1998), *Hunter's Moon* (1999), *Midnight Come Again* (2000), *The Singing of the Dead* (2001), *A Fine and Bitter Snow* (2002), *A Grave Denies* (2003), and *A Taint in the Blood* (2004).

Subject headings: Artifacts; Drugs; Oil

Appeal points: The setting for this novel appeals to readers who enjoy an exotic, but very cold, environment. Kate is a complex character who can be quietly stoic at one point and vibrant at another. She appeals to readers who are looking for a hero.

> **Readalikes**
>
> Nevada Barr's Anna Pigeon series—similar use of character
>
> Sue Henry's Alex Jensen and Jessie Arnold series—similar use of setting

DISCUSSION QUESTIONS

How would you describe Kate's personality? What gets her passionate? What makes her withdraw?

What changes Kate's opinion about the oil company once she sees it in action?

How cold did you feel reading this novel?

What should happen to the Native American artifacts that are unearthed on this project?

See standard questions in the Introduction for more questions.

◇◇◆◇◇

Josephine Tey
The Daughter of Time

Elizabeth MacKintosh was born in 1896 (or possibly 1897) in Inverness, Scotland. From 1915 to 1918 she attended the Royal Academy in Inverness and the Anstey Physical Training College in Birmingham. In the 1920s, she worked as a physical education teacher at various schools. Eventually, she resigned her teaching position to take care of her father and to begin a writing career. She used two pen names for her writing career: Josephine Tey (her great-great-grandmother) and Gordon Daviot. Her first novel, *The Man in the Queue* under the pseudonym Gordon Daviot (1929), introduced the character of Inspector Alan Grant. Her first novel under the Tey pseudonym, *A Shilling for Candies*, was published in 1936. Other titles are *Miss Pym Disposes* (1947), *The Franchise Affair* (1949), *Brat Farrar* (1949), *To Love and Be Wise* (1950), *Four, Five and Six* (1952), and *The Singing Sands* (1952). Besides her fiction career, MacKintosh was also a playwright. She died in 1952.

Plot summary: When Inspector Alan Grant of Scotland Yard is in the hospital recuperating from a broken leg, he becomes fascinated by a portrait of Richard III. Convinced that this man he sees in the portrait could not be as evil as others have suggested, he sets out to prove a new theory. Aided by his friend, the actress Marta Hallard, and a research assistant named Carradine who brings him the supporting materials he needs, Grant explores who Richard was and what happened to the boys in the tower.

Web site:
none
Reader's guide:
none

Publication date: 1951

Number of pages: 221

Geographic setting: England, London

Time period: 1950s

Series notes: Tey's first novel about Inspector Alan Grant was *The Man in the Queue* by Gordon Daviot. When she returned to this character, she shifted her pseudonym. Additional novels under the Tey pseudonym about Grant are *A Shilling for Candies* (1936), *To Love and Be Wise* (1950), and *The Singing Sands* (1952).

Subject headings: Richard III, King of England, 1452–1485

Appeal points: This analysis of a historic event through the eyes of a modern detective has appeal for all puzzle solvers whether they are mystery readers or not.

Readalikes
Dan Brown's *The Da Vinci Code*—similar use of historical context
Robin Maxwell's *To the Tower Born*—similar plot
Ian Pears—similar use of historical context

DISCUSSION QUESTIONS

What insights into Grant did you get from reading this novel?

How would you describe the relationship between Marta and Alan?

Did this mystery novel have enough action for you? Was it enough to watch the mind of Alan Grant "solve" this case?

Why is Grant so obsessed with Richard III?

What role does Carradine play in this novel?

Why do we still care about what happened so long ago?

After reading this novel, what do you think? Did Richard III kill his two nephews and have them buried in the Tower of London in order to eliminate all possible contenders for the throne?

See standard questions in the Introduction for more questions.

◇◇◆◇◇

Ngúgí wa Thiong'o

Petals of Blood

Ngúgí wa Thiong'o (known as Ngúgí) was born in 1938 in Kamiriithu, near Limuru, Kiambu District, while Kenya was a British-ruled colony. He was the fifth child of the third of his father's four wives. Raised Christian in an African environment, he was educated at Makerere University in Kampala, Uganda, and the University of Leeds. His writing often reflects the conflict between his Gikuyu heritage and his Christian/Western upbringing. Ngúgí worked as a reporter, and lectured at various colleges. In 1977 he was arrested for his writing, which was viewed by the now-independent Kenyan government as a threat. Held for one year without a trial, Ngúgí was released but not reinstated at the university, so he went into exile in 1982. From this point forward, he began to use Gikuyu, his native tongue, as his primary language in his writings. Ngúgí taught at Yale University before he became professor of comparative literature and performance studies at New York University in 1992, where he held the Erich Maria Remarque Chair.

Plot summary: This novel begins with the knowledge that three owners of the Theng'eta Breweries and Enterprises, Ltd., have been murdered. The police arrest three individuals who may be connected to the crime, while a fourth suspect lies injured in the hospital. The balance of the book is the story of the four suspects: the struggling teacher, the wounded revolutionary, the disillusioned social activist, and the lonely prostitute—who have settled in the rural village of Ilmorog to escape from the world. Told from various points of view over the twelve years leading up to the murders, the novel reveals the harsh realities and disappointments of life in independent Kenya, struggling to join the contemporary world without sacrificing its deep-rooted Kenyan traditions and beliefs.

Publication date: 1977
Number of pages: 410
Geographic setting: Kenya, Ilmorog
Time period: 1960s, 1970s
Series notes: This is a stand-alone novel. The author has written other novels about issues of colonialisms and the emergence of an African perspective from former colonies.
Subject headings: Colonialism; Kenya—Politics and government

Web site:
none
Reader's guide:
none

Readalikes

Chinua Achebe's *Things Fall Apart*—similar use of plot and setting

Chinua Achebe's *No Longer at Ease*—similar use of plot and setting

J. M. Coetzee's *Waiting for the Barbarians*—similar use of plot and setting

Joseph Conrad's *Heart of Darkness*—similar use of plot and setting

Tsitsi Dangarembga's *Nervous Conditions*—similar use of plot and setting

Stanlake Samkange's *On Trial for My Country*—similar use of plot and setting

Appeal points: This novel appeals to readers who wish to be challenged by the writing itself. The novel is dense, poetic at times in its style, and uses rapidly changing points of view to drive home the point of the similarity and differences among the characters. It shares many characteristics with classic satires, and at times reads like a parable from the Bible.

DISCUSSION QUESTIONS

Why does Chui choose not to Africanize the Siriana School after Fraudsham's departure?

Why does Munira's family see him as a failure?

Why does Ilmorog initially reject Munira's attempts to teach their children?

Why does Munira find "this secret pleasure at the illusion of being one of them"? (p. 22)

Why does the author use a twelve-year separation in time between the meeting of these characters and the eventual murders?

Why is Munira's failure at the first school rebellion so important?

Do the author's political views overshadow the story?

How true is Munira's statement (p. 141) "that man's estate is rotten at heart"?

How would you define and defend Wanja?

Told like a parable, what lessons are we to learn from the villager's journey to the city?

Are the characters from Ilmorog each "a prisoner of past defeat" (p. 273)?

Is it true that our only choice is "eat or be eaten"?

See standard questions in the Introduction for more questions.

◇◇◆◇◇

Charles Todd

A Test of Wills

Charles Todd is the joint writing name of Caroline Todd and her son Charles. Caroline Todd earned a B.A. in English literature and history and an M.A. in international relations. Charles earned a B.A. in communication studies. They live on the East Coast of the United States. They have written one stand-alone novel, *The Murder Stone* (2003).

Plot summary: Scotland Yard Detective Ian Rutledge returns from the battlefields of World War I a damaged man. Haunted by the ghost of a soldier he executed on the battlefield, he must hide his psychological scars from his superiors while he tries to regain his balance and retain his job. Sent to Upper Streetham where a veteran officer, Colonel Charles Harris, has been murdered, Rutledge discovers the chief suspect is a decorated veteran named Mark Wilton who is a friend of the Prince of Wales. Knowing that he is being set up by his superiors, Rutledge battles his demons to discover the truth.

> **Web site:**
> http://www.charlestodd.com
> **Reader's guide:**
> none

Publication date: 1996
Number of pages: 282
Geographic setting: England, Warwickshire, Upper Streetham
Time period: 1920s
Series notes: This is the first novel in the series. The other books are *Wings of Fire* (1998), *Search the Dark* (1999), *Legacy of the Dead* (2000), *Watcher's of Time* (2001), *A Fearsome Doubt* (2002), and *A Cold Treachery* (2005).

Subject headings: Veterans; World War I

Appeal points: This novel was an Anthony and Edgar nominee and a Barry Award winner for best first novel of the year. It uses an elegant style to masterfully tell a mystery story. The tremendous power of this novel is sustained by the psychologically wounded hero who battles against himself to overcome.

> **Readalikes**
>
> Rennie Airth's Inspector John Madden series—similar use of character
> James Lee Burke's Billy Bob Holland series—similar use of character

DISCUSSION QUESTIONS

What is Bowles' reason for treating a hero like Rutledge so poorly?

Why can Rutledge not get the help he needs?

Should Rutledge be haunted by Hamish?

Do you believe that Hamish is a ghost, or is he a figment of Rutledge's disorder?

What would cure Rutledge?

Will Rutledge end up like Daniel Hickam?

See standard questions in the Introduction for more questions.

◇◇◆◇◇

Mary Willis Walker

The Red Scream

Mary Willis was born in Fox Point, Wisconsin, in 1942. She earned a B.A. in English from Duke University in 1964. From 1967 until 1978 Mary taught school. She was married, had two children, and divorced. She is now a full-time writer. Her first novel, *Zero at the Bone* (1991), won the Agatha and Macavity awards as the best first mystery novel of the year. Walker lives in Austin, Texas.

Plot summary: Molly Cates is a journalist whose first book, the true crime story of serial killer Louie Bronk, has just been published. To bring closure to the story, Molly wants to cover Bronk's execution. Her editor discourages her,

Web site:
none
Reader's guide:
none

and she is warned off by millionaire contractor Charlie McFarland, the widower of Bronk's last victim. Tiny McFarland's murder is the conviction that will allow the state to kill Bronk, but Molly begins to develop doubts that he had anything to do with Tiny's death. Then a copycat murderer appears and a second death occurs.

Publication date: 1994

Number of pages: 324

Geographic setting: Texas, Austin

Time period: 1990s

Series notes: This is the first novel in the Molly Cates series. The other two are *Under the Beetle's Cellar* (1995) and *All the Dead Lie Down* (1998).

Subject headings: Death penalty; Journalists; Serial killers

Appeal points: This novel won the Edgar and Hammett awards as the best mystery novel of the year. The dogged nature of a journalist

Readalikes
Edna Buchanan's Britt Montero series—similar use of character
Jan Burke's Irene Kelly series—similar use of character
Thomas Harris' Hannibal Lechter series—similar use of serial killer plot

like Cates appeals to many readers. The thrill of reading about a serial killer is enhanced here by the poetry he writes that haunts the text.

DISCUSSION QUESTIONS

What does this book tell us about the relationship between mothers and daughters?

What role does Grady Traynor play in this story?

What fascinates us about serial killers?

What effect did Bronk's poetry have on you?

Should people like Molly write books about people like Bronk?

Should people like Bronk be put to death?

See standard questions in the Introduction for more questions.

◇◇◆◇◇

Minette Walters

Minette Walters was born in 1949 in Bishop's Stortford, England, the daughter of an army captain and an artist. Minette graduated from Durham University. In 1978 she married Alec Walters and they have two sons. She worked as an editor in London for *IPC Magazine*, a romantic-fiction publication, writing articles, short stories, and novelettes for the publication. She then became a freelance writer for numerous women's magazines. After her second son began full-time school, Walters began to write her first novel. She has been a full-time writer ever since. Her first five books were adapted for television by the BBC. In addition to her books featured below, Walters has written *The Tinder Box* (1999), *Acid Row* (2001—shortlisted for the Gold Dagger Award and for the Grand Prix des Lectrices de Elle, France), *Fox Evil* (2002—winner of the Gold Dagger Award), *Disordered Minds* (2003), and *Devil's Feather* (2005). She lives in an eighteenth-century manor house in Dorchester in Dorset.

> **Web site:**
> http://www.minettewalters.co.uk

The Breaker

Plot summary: When Kate Sumner's body washes ashore at Dorset, it becomes apparent she has been drugged, raped, and thrown in the sea to drown. Equally chilling, her three-year-old daughter Hannah is found wandering the streets of the town of Poole. As the police investigate, credible suspects surface, ranging from the victim's husband William, a randy actor named Steven Harding, and a teacher named Tony Bridges. The case is investigated from two different angles when the outsider Detective Inspector John Galbraith matches wits with the local constable Nick Ingram. Ingram finds himself attracted to Maggie Jenner, a local stable owner who has fallen on hard times. As each lie in the case is exposed, the detectives get one step closer to understanding the horror of this crime.

> **Reader's guide:**
> none

Publication date: 1998
Number of pages: 355
Geographic setting: England, Dorset
Time period: 1990s
Series notes: This is a stand-alone novel.
Subject headings: Children at risk; Sailing
Appeal points: This psychological work masterfully sets up three major suspects. Walters' real talent is in the painfully slow way she reveals the truth in her novels.

> **Readalikes**
>
> Elizabeth George's Thomas Lynley series—similar use of character
>
> Val McDermid's *A Place of Execution*—similar use of plot
>
> Ruth Rendell—similar use of psychological suspense

DISCUSSION QUESTIONS

Why is Kate's home adorned only with pictures of herself?

William claims he only married Kate for the sex (p. 232). Do you believe him?

How is Hannah capable of walking all the way back to the harbor after Steve dumps her off?

Why does Hannah hide the shoes?

Why does Hannah abuse herself in front of the police officer?

Why does Hannah scream at William until the moment that Steven Harding is arrested?

Why does Galbraith feel compelled to save William Sumner?

Galbraith thinks (p. 90), "Sociopaths could be as charming and as unthreatening as the rest of humanity, and it was always a potential victim who thought otherwise." Who is a sociopath in this novel and why?

How does Vivienne Purdy's reaction to her husband's infidelity (p. 207) differ from Maggie Jenner's reaction to Martin Grant's (Robert Healey) crimes?

Galbraith says (p. 247) "he thought of himself in the role of a priest offering a kind of benediction merely by listening, but he had neither the authority nor the desire to forgive sins." Do we ask too much of our police detectives?

Is Ingram a romantic, a mystic, or a stoic? What is the fate of the courtship of Nick and Maggie?

Galbraith says (p. 73), "You can be loved too much as well as too little, you know, and I'd be hard-pushed to say which was the most dangerous." What would you say?

What is the fate of Hannah after this novel ends?

See standard questions in the Introduction for more questions.

◇◇◆◇◇

The Dark Room

Plot summary: Jinx Kingsley has been found wandering around an abandoned airfield, apparently after trying to kill herself. And why not? Her husband was murdered ten years ago. Recently, her new fiancé Leo and her best friend Meg have cheated on her, and they have both been murdered. Jinx is the logical suspect. With her memory of the recent crucial days lost, she turns to Dr. Alan Protheroe for help.

Reader's guide:
none

Publication date: 1998
Number of pages: 381
Geographic setting: England, London
Time period: 1990s
Series notes: This is a stand-alone novel.
Subject headings: Amnesia; Photography
Appeal points: This novel was shortlisted for the Gold Dagger Award. This is a psychological novel that probes into the psyche of the character in order to reveal the crime.

Readalikes
Elizabeth George's Thomas Lynley series—similar use of character
Ruth Rendell—similar use of psychological suspense

DISCUSSION QUESTIONS

Did you believe Jinx had amnesia?

What characteristics does Jinx have that would keep her from committing suicide?

Does Jinx really find Dr. Alan Protheroe attractive, or is she just unaware of her own dependence on him?

Does Jinx understand what happened to her dead husband?

What role does Jinx's father play in her story?

How did the secondary story about the prostitutes fit in this story?

Does Meg deserve her fate?

Does Leo deserve his fate?

Is there "a difference between justice and revenge"?

See standard questions in the Introduction for more questions.

◇◇◆◇◇

The Echo

Plot summary: When a homeless man named Billy Blake is found dead in the garage of successful architect Amanda Powell, journalist Michael Deacon begins to probe into the reasons why Blake would choose to starve to death in front of a well-stocked refrigerator. As it is revealed that Blake might have been a banker who disappeared with an enormous fortune, the mystery deepens. What happened to the banker's wife? And how does all of this relate to the stoic Amanda Powell?

Publication date: 1997

Reader's guide:
none

Readalikes

George Dawes Green's *The Caveman's Valentine*—similar use of challenged character

Laurie R. King's *To Play the Fool*—similar use of challenged character

---

Number of pages: 338
Geographic setting: England, London
Time period: 1990s
Series notes: This is a stand-alone novel.
Subject headings: Homeless; Journalists
Appeal points: This novel is based on the Oedipal myth. The truth about the characters is revealed through the painful psychological probing of the characters, including the lead investigator. There are no heroes in this novel.

DISCUSSION QUESTIONS

Why does Billy Blake die in Amanda Powell's' garage?

Why does Billy Blake burn his hands?

How does Billy Blake know Amanda Powell is a murderer?

Why does Amanda Powell murder the first time?

Why does Amanda Powell murder the second time?

Who has the money? (Who is the weeping woman in South Africa?)

Why does Michael Deacon care about Amanda; Terry; Lawrence; and Barry?

Should Michael forgive his mother?

Is Lawrence the puppet master for this whole set of events?

React to the quote: "This is the end of the twentieth century and people don't have consciences anymore. They have clever solicitors instead."

See standard questions in the Introduction for more questions.

◇◇◆◇◇

The Ice House

Reader's guide:
none

Plot summary: Phoebe Maybury is living in Streech Grange with her lesbian companions—interior designer Diana Goode and journalist Anna Cattrell. Phoebe's long-missing ex-husband had abused their daughter and disappeared. When a corpse is found in an unused icehouse on the property, Chief Inspector Walsh focuses his investigation on Phoebe. And why not? He suspected her of foul play ten years ago when her husband disappeared.

Publication date: 1992
Number of pages: 240
Geographic setting: England, Hampshire
Time period: 1990s
Series notes: This is a stand-alone novel.
Subject heading: Lesbianism
Appeal points: This is Walter's first novel, and it was the winner of the John Creasey Award for the Best First Crime Novel of the year.

> **Readalikes**
>
> Donna Leon's *Death at La Fenice*—similar use of plot and theme

DISCUSSION QUESTIONS

How much of Phoebe's life should be dictated by her ex-husband's actions?

Should Phoebe have stayed at Streech Grange? Would her life have been any different if she had moved?

How fair can Inspector Walsh be to Phoebe considering their history?

What would cause a village to consider these three women a coven of witches?

What role does Diana Goode play in the novel?

What role does Anne Cattrell play in the novel?

What is at the core of the relationship between Anne and Detective Sergeant McLoughlin?

What is the role of Maisie Thompson in the novel?

See standard questions in the Introduction for more questions.

◇◦━◆━◦◇

The Scold's Bridle

Plot summary: When Mathilda Gillespie is found dead in her bathtub, her head is encased in a scold's bridle. Oddly, she has bequeathed her fortune to her doctor, Sarah Blakeney, instead of her hated daughter Joanna or unreliable granddaughter Ruth. Even Blakeney's never-do-well husband Jack gets dragged into this investigation by Detective Sergeant Cooper. It becomes the task of the doctor to prove that she is innocent of murder.

> **Reader's guide:**
> none

Publication date: 1994

Number of pages: 327
Geographic setting: England, Dorset, Fontwell
Time period: 1990s
Series notes: This is a stand-alone novel.
Subject headings: Children at risk; Inheritence; Wills

Appeal points: This novel won the Gold Dagger Award for best crime novel of the year. Despite the psychological stresses within the plot, this novel appeals to readers who enjoy a small English-village mystery.

Readalikes

Ruth Rendell—similar use of psychological suspense

DISCUSSION QUESTIONS

Does Mathilda Gillespie deserve her fate?

What purpose does the "scold's bridle" serve in this story?

Why is Dr. Sarah Blakeney the only woman who can relate to Mathilda?

Why does Sarah tolerate Jack? What took her so long to get a divorce?

Is Mathilda responsible for how her daughter Joanna turned out?

Why does Mathilda cling to her granddaughter Ruth?

How responsible is Ruth, considering her fate?

Is there any kind of appropriate punishment for Mathilda's father?

See standard questions in the Introduction for more questions.

◇◆◇

The Sculptress

Reader's guide:
none

Plot summary: Convicted of chopping up her mother and sister with an axe, Olive Martin is passing her life in prison carving human figures out of wax. When her publisher suggests there may be a book in Olive's story, writer Rosalind Leigh grudgingly decides to interview Olive. Once she meets Olive, Roz is drawn into her cell repeatedly as she begins to redefine what is the truth surrounding this case.

Publication date: 1993
Number of pages: 308
Geographic setting: England
Time period: 1990s
Series notes: This is a stand-alone novel.

Subject headings: Convicts; Journalists

Appeal points: This novel won the Macavity Award and Edgar Allan Poe Award for best novel of the year. Olive is one of the scariest fictional characters ever, and Walters does a masterful job of describing her to the reader. This is a very disturbing novel to read, in a sense sharing the same emotional appeal as horror fiction.

Readalikes
Elizabeth George's *A Great Deliverance*—similar use of plot
Thomas Harris' *The Silence of the Lambs*—similar use of plot

DISCUSSION QUESTIONS

The classic mystery pattern is to see a murder, have a detective, have a hunt, and have a resolution. Suspense is simply about what happens next—and being anxious about it. So what kind of book did we read?

What characteristics does this novel share with other types of fiction genres?

What appeals to us in a creepy story like this?

What made us feel creepy when we were reading this book?

Were there any characters that you liked?

Were there any characters you felt sorry for?

Regarding Alice's death, who is guilty?

What are Roz's motivations for writing about Olive?

What would make you believe that Olive has magical powers?

Why does Olive bust up her cell?

What was there about the romance that appealed to you?

Why do you think the author wrote this book?

What is this book's theme?

See standard questions in the Introduction for more questions.

◇◇◆◇◇

The Shape of Snakes

Plot summary: M. Ranelagh, who has been on a twenty-year mission to explain the death of her neighbor on Graham Road, "Mad Annie" Butts, narrates this story. It was M. who found Butts dying in a gutter one night following months of abuse at the hands of her neighbors due to Butts' Tourette's syndrome and alcoholism. Driven by a

Reader's guide:
none

sense of justice and a need for revenge, M. pursues a line of investigation that puts her own family situation at risk and sets neighbor against neighbor as each truth is revealed.

Publication date: 2001

Number of pages: 371

Geographic setting: England, Dorset, Dorchester; England, London

Time period: 1970s, 1990s

Series notes: This is a stand-alone novel.

Subject headings: Race relations; Revenge; Tourette's syndrome

Appeal points: This novel won the Pelle Rosencrantz Prize from Denmark. It appeals to readers who do not mind an untrustworthy narrator. The power of this novel is the way it displays the suffering of middle- and lower-class people who are struggling to survive. Cruelty to animals is a minor subplot in the story, which will not appeal to all readers.

Readalikes

Daniel Hecht's *Skull Session*—similar use of plot

Jonathan Lethem's *Motherless Brooklyn*—similar use of plot

Laura Lippman's *The Last Place*—similar use of plot

DISCUSSION QUESTIONS

Is it wise for any community to place "council-owned properties" in neighborhoods that do not want them?

Was "Mad Annie" unlovable? Was she less deserving of love because she was different?

Should there be an "element of compulsion in the treatment of vulnerable people" (p. 5)?

What should be done about Alan Slater and Michael Percy?

Is M. manipulative for the good, or for the bad?

What characteristics does M. share with her mother?

Has M. ever loved Sam?

How is it true "that control rests with whomever worries least about being seen to exercise it"? Why does M.'s lip have a tic?

How is "revenge an unworthy ambition"? How can it be confused with justice?

How guilty should Sam feel about his actions on the night Annie died?

How many tragedies in this novel can be blamed on men having sexual power over women?

See standard questions in the Introduction for more questions.

◇◆◇

Larry Watson

Montana 1948

Larry Watson was born in 1947 in Rugby, North Dakota, the son of a sheriff. He has a B.A. and an M.A. from the University of North Dakota. Watson earned a Ph.D. in the creative-writing program at the University of Utah. He taught writing and literature at the University of Wisconsin-Stevens Point from 1979 until 2004. He is currently a visiting professor at Marquette University. Besides this title, Watson wrote *In a Dark Time* (1980), *Justice* (1995), *White Crosses* (1997), *Laura* (2000), and *Orchard* (2003). He lives with his wife Susan in rural Wisconsin; they have two daughters.

Plot summary: Wesley Hayden is the sheriff of the small Montana town of Bentrock in 1948. His brother Frank is a returned war hero and the town's doctor. When the sheriff's maid, Marie Little Soldier, a Sioux, proves reluctant to be seen by Frank, Wesley begins to suspect that all is not well in this community. Later, Marie is found dead, and Wesley is forced to make a difficult choice. All of the complex maneuverings in this small town are witnessed by the twelve-year-old David Hayden, Wesley's son, including a crucial clue that may determine if murder occurred.

> **Web site:**
> http://larry-watson.com
>
> **Reader's guide:**
> http://www.simonsays.com/content/content.cfm?sid=33&pid=404713&agid=10

Publication date: 1993

Number of pages: 175

Geographic setting: Montana, Bentrock

Time period: 1940s

Series notes: This is a stand-alone novel.

Subject headings: Coming of age; Native Americans

Appeal points: This novel received the Milkweed National Fiction Prize. This literary coming-of-age novel uses its Western setting and its time period to help drive home the story. The moral dilemma over the rape of marginalized women is a complex issue that troubles some readers.

> **Readalikes**
>
> Harper Lee's *To Kill a Mockingbird*—similar coming-of-age novel
>
> Robert R. McCammon's *A Boy's Life*—similar coming-of-age novel

DISCUSSION QUESTIONS

This story is narrated by a twelve-year-old boy. Why is he an effective narrator?

David reveals many thoughts and emotions to us in the novel. Name some and define them as right or wrong.

David speculates that it is both character and practicality that kept his father from wearing his badge. Why do you think Wesley never wore a badge?

Why does Wes fear his father?

Why does Wes say yes when his father tells him to be sheriff?

How intentional is Julian's slight of Wes at the ceremony?

David speculates his grandfather wanted to be sheriff because "he needed power." Can you site examples of this need?

How much does Julian know?

Why does Frank molest the women that he does?

David says Marie specializes in telling outrageous lies. Is she a credible witness against Frank?

Why does Wes not want to believe the accusations against Frank at first?

When Wes hears of Frank's battlefield heroism, he says, "I wonder if he was supposed to stay at the hospital?" What does that statement tell us about the relationship between the brothers?

How would you characterize the relationship between the white population and the Native Americans?

Can the differences between the races ever be bridged?

Are the Highdogs paid to collect the golf balls, or are they "selling them back" as a crime?

Why does Wes keep Frank in the basement rather than jailing him?

Why does Frank break the canning jars?

Did Frank murder Marie Little Soldier?

Does Wes murder Frank?

David calls his folks "hapless." Are they really?

How many secrets can one town keep?

Does Pandora's box still exist in this town?

See standard questions in the Introduction for more questions.

◇◇◆◇◇

Robert Wilson

A Small Death in Lisbon

Robert Wilson was born in 1957. After graduating from Oxford University in 1979 with a degree in English, he worked in Crete leading archaeological tours and as an advertising man in a business agency. He has also lived and worked in Africa. He is the author of the Bruce Medway series including *Instruments of Darkness* (1995), *The Big Killing* (1996), *Blood Is Dirt* (1997), and *A Darkening Stain* (1997). He is also the author of *A Company of Strangers* (2001), *The Blind Man of Seville* (2003), and *The Vanished Hands* (2004).

Plot summary: In 1941, German industrialist Klaus Felsen is forced to go to Lisbon and return with wolfram (tungsten) for the Nazi war effort. In 1999, when Catarina Oliviera, the daughter of a prominent lawyer, is found murdered on the beach in Lisbon, police inspector Ze Coehlo is given the case. Eventually, these two disparate incidents draw together the story of Portugal and how it suffered in the 1940s, the 1970s, and today.

Web site:
none
Reader's guide:
none

Publication date: 2000

Number of pages: 440

Geographic setting: Portugal, Lisbon

Time period: 1940s, 1990s

Series notes: This is a stand-alone novel.

Subject heading: Nazi Germany

Appeal points: This novel won the Gold Dagger award for best crime novel of the year. It reveals an aspect of World War II that will be little known, and does it in the unique setting of Portugal, a country that was neutral during the war, had a revolution in the 1970s, and continues to react to those factors today. Felsen's story is not pretty, and some readers may be uncomfortable with his character.

Readalikes
Graham Greene—similar literary style
Philip Kerr's Bernie Gunther series—similar use of a character in a historical setting
John Le Carre—similar literary style in an espionage plot

DISCUSSION QUESTIONS

The theme of this book is betrayal. Name the major characters and whom they betrayed and who betrayed them.

Did you enjoy the author's style (mixing the past and present time periods, alternating between first and third person, lyrical choice of words and phrases)?

Felsen says of Eva, "all he could think of was how Eva had taught him nothing, tried to teach him the mystery of nothing, the intricacies of space between words and lines. She was a great withholder." Did it surprise you that she would harbor Jewish refugees?

Felsen says, "He walked slowly out of the building contemplating his first lesson in underestimating the Portuguese." Why is he incapable of seeing the truth?

Why is Felsen so emotionally scarred by the murder of Edward Burton?

Ze says, "It's a stomach thing for me, police work. For a lot of my colleagues it's brain work. They have suspects, the clues, the statements, the witnesses, the motives and they reason them all together. I do that too but I have something in my stomach as well, something that tells me if I'm right. Antonio Borrego once asked me what it was like and the only thing I could think of was 'love' and he told me to be careful because, as anyone knows, love is blind. Good point. It's not like love, but that's the strength of it." How good a detective is Ze?

How many characters can you name that really love?

Are Antonio Borrego's acts justified?

What motivates Felsen to murder the Nazis Lehrer, Hanke, Fischer, and Wolff?

See standard questions in the Introduction for more questions.

◇◇◆◇◇

Jacqueline Winspear

Maisie Dobbs

Jacqueline Winspear was born in 1955 in Kent, England. She attended the University of London's Institute of Education. Subsequently, Winspear worked in the academic publishing industry in London, as well as in higher education and in the marketing communications business. In 1990 she moved to California to take up a fiction writing career. She won the Agatha Award and the Independent Mystery Booksellers Association's Dilys Award for *Birds of a Feather*. She is married and lives in Ojai, California.

> **Web site:**
> http://www.jacquelinewinspear.com
> **Reader's guide:**
> none

Plot summary: Maisie Dobbs is hired by Christopher Davenham to follow his wife Celia when he believes she is having an affair. As Maisie follows Celia to the grave of a World War I casualty, it brings home the state of affairs in London ten years after the war to end all wars. The book at this point takes a diversion into Maisie's youth, chronicling her rise from the poor Lambreth district in southeast London. Maisie is the much loved daughter of Frankie Dobbs, a costermonger who is not above trading her to Lady Rowan Compton to work as an in-between maid. Through a series of circumstances, Maisie receives an education above her station and status when she becomes Lady Compton's protégée. A college education leads to an avocation as a nurse. When World War I intervenes, a series of events sends her to France and a bittersweet love affair. Winspear manages to blend the sad story of combat injuries and lost love with the current case ten years later.

Publication date: 2003

Number of pages: 294

Geographic setting: England, London; France

Time period: 1910s, 1920s

Series notes: This is the first book in the series. The additional titles are *Birds of a Feather* (2004) and *Pardonable Lies* (2005). This book is much more than a mystery, covering a great deal of the back story of the character. That should appeal to readers of historical novels, but it may not thrill readers just looking for a mystery. The carefully crafted historical details should appeal to all readers.

Subject headings: Veterans; World War I

Appeal points: *Maisie Dobbs* won the Agatha and Macavity awards for Best First Novel and was nominated for the Edgar Allan Poe Award for Best Novel (rare for a first novel to be nominated in this category). The novel was

> **Readalikes**
>
> Rhys Bowen's Molly Murphy series—similar use of a character in a historical setting
>
> Dianne Day's Fremont Jones series—similar use of a character in a historical setting

also a New York Times Notable Book 2003, a Publishers' Weekly Top Ten Mystery 2003, and a BookSense Top Ten selection. Because Winspear's grandfather was severely wounded and shell-shocked at the Battle of the Somme in 1916, there is a special poignancy to the development of the soldiers in this novel. Dobbs' struggles to gain her own personal freedoms mirrors the rise of women's rights and should appeal for its historical significance. This novel reads at times like a romance, and it also works as a historical novel of dynamic proportions.

DISCUSSION QUESTIONS

How would you describe this novel: romance, historical, mystery, or...?

How would you describe Maisie as a child?

What role does Lady Rowan Compton play in Maisie's life? What would Maisie's life have been like if she had not worked for her?

What does Dr. Basil Khan give to Maisie that helps her through life?

What attributes do Maisie and Celia Davenham share?

Who is more important in Maisie's life: Frankie Dobbs or Billy Beale?

How proficient a detective is Maisie? Is this a play fair mystery?

How would you define "the forensic science of the whole person"?

What did the author do to convince you of the consequences of combat on individuals?

How evil is The Retreat?

How tragic is the story of Dr. Simon Lynch?

See standard questions in the Introduction for more questions.

◇◇◆◇◇

50 Additional Mystery and Crime Fiction Books to Consider for Discussions

Brigitte Aubert

Death from the Woods

Elise Andrioli is the blind, mute, and quadriplegic victim of an Irish terrorist bomb living out her life in a small suburb outside of Paris. Someone is mutilating and murdering young boys. Elise is drawn in when a young girl named Virginie tells her that she witnessed "Death from the Woods" murder one of the victims, news that Virginie reveals prior to the discovery of the boy's body. Why does this young witness choose the damaged woman as her confessor? How will Elise overcome her challenges to communicate to the investigator assigned to the case? Told from Elise's point of view, this novel won the Grand Prix de Littérature Policière of France and was a Penzler Pick. (1997)

Jo Bannister

Reflections

Brodie Farrell runs a business called "Looking for Something?", which is located in Northern Ireland. In her third case, an uncle hires Farrell to find his niece Constance. The question is whether Constance would be willing to adopt her two sisters, Juanita and Emerald Daws. Their father, Robert, has murdered their mother, Serena. While Farrell hunts, she leaves the children in the care of her teacher friend Daniel Hood, who proves challenged by the task and is placed at risk because of it. Eventually the police investigation led by cop Jack Deacon and the private investigation led by Farrell merge at the conclusion of this psychological thriller. (2003)

Robert Bausch

The Gypsy Man

John Bone is sent to prison for the accidental murder of a young black girl from his Virginia mountain home of Crawford in 1953. While he languishes in prison, a fellow prisoner named P. J. "Peach" Middleton escapes. The author uses multiple points of view to show how, in 1959, the community still suffers the echoes of crimes blamed on an old mountain legend, the Gypsy Man, including the death of another black child named Terry Landon. John's wife Penny worries about the safety of her own child, not knowing that Peach is stalking her aunt Clare. Eventually all the separate stories are brought together to reveal the effect of love and self-reliance on even the most evil of actions. (2002)

Rhys Bowen

Murphy's Law

While defending her honor, Irish lass Molly Murphy accidentally kills her landlord's son and must flee her native land for America. Landing in Tammany Hall-era New York, circumstances have made her the guardian of two small children and a suspect in the death of a man from her ship who dies on Ellis Island. New York policeman Daniel Sullivan is on her side, but this situation is going to require her to investigate on her own. This is the first book in a series of novels about this character. *Murphy's Law* was selected for the Agatha and Herodotus awards for best novel of the year and was a Mary Higgins Clark Award finalist. (2001)

C. J. Box

Open Season

Joe Pickett is a Wyoming game warden and in this series debut he must confront his worst fears. The county of Twelve Sleep where he lives with his pregnant wife and their daughters has not been hospitable, to the point where he loses his own gun to a local poacher. When that same man ends up dead in Joe's backyard, his life begins to unravel and his family is placed in danger. The death reveals a need to protect an endangered species while trying to keep a rural arena from bursting into flames. *Open Season* won the Anthony, Barry, Gumshoe, and Macavity awards for best first mystery novel, was short listed for the Edgar Award, and was selected by the New York Times, L.A. Times Book Prize, and Penzler Pick as one of the best novels of the year. (2001)

John Burdett

Bangkok 8

Detective Sonchai Jitpleecheep of the Royal Thai Police Force is given the assignment of finding the murderer of U.S. Marine Sergeant William Bradley. Bradley was killed in Bangkok by the same snake that was used to kill Jitpleecheep's cop partner Pichai Apiradee. This flat-out thriller reveals the dark underbelly of Thailand's major city, including its drug problems, sexual trade, and smuggling markets. Throughout the book, the Buddhist beliefs of the devout detective help reveal the soul of this country's culture and how he deals with his own complex racial heritage. (2003)

Michael Chabon

The Final Solution: A Story of Detection

The Old Man (read: Sherlock Holmes) has retired to raise bees in peace, but during the summer of 1944 a small mute boy named Linus Steinman shows up in Sussex where the eighty-nine-year-old lives. With the mute is an African gray parrot who recites numbers in German, and when the bird is stolen and a man is killed, the local police want an explanation from the Grand Master. This novella has respect for the traditions established by Arthur Conan Doyle and pushes the classic mystery into the world of contemporary literature. It won the Aga Khan Prize for Fiction. (2004)

Jeffery Deaver

The Bone Collector

Lincoln Rhyme is a quadriplegic known as the world's foremost criminalist. Forced by his condition to utilize technology to uncover the clues, he is aided by Amelia Sachs, a policewoman who suffers with arthritis. In this case, he matches wits with a serial killer who murders his victims by gruesome methods found in a book about the criminal life rampant in old New York. This novel is an example of a flat-out thriller written by a master of this style. This is the first book in a series about Rhyme. (1997)

John Gregory Dunne

True Confessions

The Virgin Tramp is found brutalized in an empty lot in 1940s Los Angeles. When her death becomes a media circus, two brothers are dragged into the investigation. Homicide Lieutenant Tom Spellacy is a cop dedicated to finding the murderer in a city not prone to revealing its truths. The Right Reverend Monsignor Desmond Spellacy is a priest in a Church hierarchy that may have a reason to keep the truth from seeing the light of day. Whether either brother will be able to sustain his loyalty to each other becomes a crucial question in this novel. (1977)

Umberto Eco

The Name of the Rose

Brother William of Baskerville, a Benedictine monk, has been sent to a Franciscan monastery in Italy to solve a murder in the year 1327. While he investigates, seven more deaths occur, and it appears that the murderer is trying to send a message to the abbey from the Book of Revelation. This novel was a nominee for the Edgar Award for Best Novel. (1983)

Jasper Fforde
The Eyre Affair

Here is a mystery within the fantasy genre. England is a police state in 1985, and the country has been fighting a war for over 130 years. On the positive side, the nation is obsessed with its literature. The nation's third most-wanted criminal is Acheron Hades, who is capable of stealing beloved literary characters from their books and holding them for ransom. The nation's response from its Special Operations Network is to form a Literary Division with star agent Thursday Next. With Hades focusing on *Jane Eyre*, Next must stay one step ahead of the kidnapper to keep the characters from disappearing forever. *The Eyre Affair* was a Penzler Pick. (2002)

Claire Francis
Deceit

When a yacht goes missing at sea for months, it takes former Parliament member Harry Richmond with it. Left behind is his wife Ellen, who wants to believe her troubled husband committed suicide over political and financial difficulties. But Harry's military friend Richard Moreland believes Harry was murdered, and as he pursues an unwanted investigation, tension ensues. Is Ellen a mother trying to protect her children or is she trying to hide her own guilt? (2001)

Alan Furst
Kingdom of Shadows

Nicholas Morath is an expatriated Hungarian aristocrat living in pre–World War II Paris when his uncle, Count Janos Polanyi, enlists him to carry secret documents needed by the resistance to the Hungarian Fascists in power in the old country. Morath is forced to ally himself with a dangerous band of people, including both friends and enemies, whose increasing desperation mirrors the historical events sealing Europe's fate. As Nicholas proceeds to carry out the Count's requests, he finds himself drawn into the political intrigue that will soon cast Europe into a long and bloody conflict. *Kingdom of Shadows* was a Penzler Pick. (2001)

Joseph Geary

Spiral

Nick Greer is a biographer in search of the story of controversial British artist Frank Spira. Five years of work is coming to an end despite missing a crucial interview with Jacob Grossman, the man rumored to be Spira's lover. When Grossman is located in Manhattan, Greer gets his witness to talk. Then Grossman is killed and Greer becomes a suspect in the murder. What is the secret of the lost painting known as *The Incarnation*? What is the connection to the mystical land of Tangiers? (2003)

Bartholomew Gill

Death in Dublin

This is the sixteenth novel to feature the cases of Peter McGarr, Chief Superintendent of the Serious Crimes Unit of the Garda Siochana. In this adventure, The Book of Kells has been stolen from the Old Library at Trinity College and is being held for ransom by a terrorist group called the New Druids. With the threat of a page a day being destroyed if the ransom is not met, McGarr savagely investigates all the relevant clues. (2003)

Carol Goodman

The Seduction of Water

Iris Greenfeder's literary career is not blossoming in New York City, so she decides to spend a summer away from the city as the manager of the old hotel in the Catskills, The Equinox, which her father managed and where her mother Katharine wrote two novels. Tragically, her mother's writing career ended when she died in a mysterious fire on Coney Island. Turning to the idea of writing a memoir of her mother, Iris tries to discover the secrets of a manuscript rumored to be her mother's third and final literary work. Her effort to uncover the secrets of her own family turns the community against her and sets her against the protectors of her mother's literary reputation. (2003)

Stephen Gray

The Artist Is a Thief

Australian Aboriginal artist Margaret Thatcher Gandarrwuy's works have always been well received and command high prices. When her latest painting is unveiled, it is discovered that the words "the artist is a thief" have been smeared across the canvas. A civil rights group hires Melbourne financial consultant Jean-Loup Wild to investigate, and as he probes into the case he finds Australia's prejudices are not far below the calm surface. (2001)

Michael Gruber
Tropic of Night

An anthropologist is fleeing her marriage to DeWitt Moore because he has become a sorcerer in a sect of shamans from Nigeria. Fearing for her life, she abandons everything to live in Miami in obscurity under the name Jane Doe. When the murder of a pregnant woman in Miami threatens her and her adopted daughter, Jane fears she has not been able to escape the reaches of her husband's power. She must join forces with a Cuban American police detective named Jimmy Paz as he hunts down the killer. (2003)

Batya Gur
A Literary Murder

Superintendent of Criminal Investigations Michael Ohayon of Jerusalem is assigned the case when two professors from the Hebrew Literature Department are killed. Iddo Dudai was suffocated in a scuba-diving accident, while Shaul Tirosh was murdered, but the two are linked because of a conflict over an academic question and a romantic entanglement. Is the solution to this crime located in the complex poems of Dr. Tirosh? (1993)

Mark Haddon
The Curious Incident of the Dog in the Night-Time

Fifteen-year-old Christopher Boone is an autistic who can master mathematics but cannot function socially, being unable to understand emotion or to be touched. When Christopher finds the neighbor's poodle Wellington stuck on a garden fork, he is accused of doing the evil deed. Released from an overnight stay in jail, Christopher sets out to become a detective like his hero Sherlock Holmes and discover who murdered the dog in the nighttime. The journal of his discoveries makes up the text. This novel was a Booker Prize and British Book Award nominee and winner of the British Book Award for Children and the Literary Fiction Award. (2003)

Erin Hart

Haunted Ground

Irish farmer Brendan McGannis, cutting in the peat bogs one day, discovers the preserved head of a red-haired woman. Trying to solve the mystery of the woman, Galway Detective Garret Devaney asks for help from archaeologist Cormac Maguire and American pathologist Nora Gavin from the Trinity College of Medicine. Living in the gothic horror Bracklyn House, owned by Hugh Osborne, the detectives find themselves housed with a man who is one of the potential suspects and whose Indian-born wife and child went missing two years ago. This novel was an Agatha Award for Best First Novel nominee and won the Romantic Times Reviewers' Choice Award for Best Mystery & Suspense—Best First Mystery. (2003)

William Heffernan

Beulah Hill

In 1930s Vermont, the murdered corpse of a racist named Royal Firman is found on Nigger Hill, known by that name because the hill is commanded by Jehiel Flood, a successful black farmer. Samuel Bradley, constable of Jerusalem's Landing, must try to solve the murder while balancing his feelings for Flood's daughter Elizabeth, the schoolmarm. Bradley is a man who lives in both the white and black world, labeled "bleached" by a state law that says that after three generations of intermingling he is now legally considered a white man. (2000)

Kathy Hepinstall

Prince of Lost Places

When an incident at the local school terrifies Martha Wells, she packs her six-year-old son Duncan in their car and moves into a remote cave on the Rio Grande. Martha's attempt to find security and peace is viewed as insanity by her husband, David, who hires private investigator William Travis to hunt her down and bring her back. When the detective begins to fall for the mother, the issue of whether she is sane or not must be confronted. (2002)

Thomas Hettche

The Arbogast Case

Convicted of causing the death of East German refugee Marie Gurst while having a mutually violent sexual experience, the notorious West German Hans Arbogast has been in prison for fifteen years. But when a crusading West German lawyer and a curious Swiss novelist combine their enquiries with a colleague on the East German side of the wall, doubts are raised about what really happened. How then to explain the strange sexual obsessions of the imprisoned Arbogast? Set in 1953 post–war Germany, this novel is based on a true crime. (2003)

Janette Turner Hospital
Due Preparations for the Plague

Air France Flight 64, hijacked by terrorists in 1987, was eventually blown up, taking the lives of a number of victims, one of whom was Lowell Hawthorne's mother. What haunts Lowell is how much his father, an American intelligence agent, knew about the hijacking before it happened. Then Lowell's father dies under suspicious circumstances and Lowell begins to get calls from one of the hijacking's survivors. (2003)

Angela Huth
Easy Silence

William Handle, the principal violinist of the Elmtree String Quartet, is happily married to his painter wife, Grace. When the quartet adds its first female member, the very attractive Bonnie Morse, William loses his head and begins to plan to get rid of Grace. Grace meanwhile is failing to see the signals because her life is invaded daily by her strange neighbor, Lucien, a man full of high-strung emotional outbursts and violent behaviors. Will a formally mild-mannered British gentleman like William really murder his wife? (1999)

Susanna Jones
The Earthquake Bird

Yorkshire born Lucy Fly is working as a translator in Tokyo when she is arrested for the murder of Lily Bridges. During extensive interviews, Lucy reveals her Yorkshire connection to Lily, her friendship with the women she has met in Japan, and her affair with the photographer Teiji. Stories of another death, a mysterious woman who only appears in photographs, and Lucy referring to herself in the third person are disturbing examples of the forces working inside Lucy. The more she reveals, the more doubts are raised in the minds of the investigators as to her actual guilt. This novel won the John Creasey Memorial Award as the best first mystery of the year. (2001)

Suki Kim

The Interpreter

Five years prior to the start of this novel, Suzy Park's parents were shot to death. Now a court interpreter for New York City who has to deal with her psychologically damaged sister and a series of bad relationships with married men, Suzy is not looking to explain the tragedy of her parents' death. But when a revealing clue falls in her lap, she must decide what to do. How will this second-generation Korean American overcome her personal difficulties to deal with this tragedy from her past? (2003)

Natsuo Kirno

Out

Yayoi works the night shift making box lunches in a Tokyo factory. There she bonds with Masako Katori, an older woman who is willing to guide her through her domestic turmoil. Yayoi will need her help when in a fit of rage she strangles her husband who has been sleeping around and gambling away all of her hard-earned money. Allied with Yoshie and Kunkio from the factory, they hide the body and begin to assemble the needed alibis for Yayoi's deadly deed. This novel was nominated for an Edgar Award as the best mystery of the year. (1997)

William Landay

Mission Flats

Ben Truman has moved from the big city to Versailles, Maine, to take care of his mother, who has Alzheimer's disease. As the new small-town police chief, he does not expect to find the body of Boston's assistant district attorney in one of the area's tourist cabins. The clues lead back to the Mission Flats area of Boston where a ten-year-old crime is still having repercussions. Battling big-city prejudice and resentment, Truman is determined to discover the truth despite the consequences. This novel won the John Creasey Memorial Award as the best mystery of the year. (2003)

Jonathan Lethem

Motherless Brooklyn

Would you hire a detective with Tourette's Syndrome? Lionel "Freakshow" Essrog was adopted out of a home for boys as a teenager by small-time hood

Frank Minna. Frank trains four wayward boys to do odd jobs for his detective agency and limousine service, not unlike Fagan. Frank teaches Freakshow to be an investigator, overlooking the barking and twitching. Hopefully Frank did a good job, because when he is murdered and dumped in a dumpster in Brooklyn, it will be Lionel who will have to do the investigation, despite being warned off by The Clients. This novel was the National Book Critics Circle Award for Fiction and Macallan Gold Dagger winner. (1999)

Michael Malone

Uncivil Seasons

Hillston, North Carolina, detectives Justin Savile and Cuddy Mangum are assigned the case when a state senator's wife is beaten to death. While they probe into the secrets of the town's ruling families, they must also try to prevent an unlikely suspect from being railroaded for the crime in order to cover up the real reason for the murder. Savile is an outcast from society, and with good humor and obsessive pep, he relishes the challenge to bring down the high and the mighty still living by an old Southern code. (1983)

Adrian McKinty

Dead I Well May Be

Michael Forsythe has escaped his homeland of Northern Ireland for a life of crime in New York City. As an enforcer for Darkey White, he becomes a killer-for-hire battling rival Dominican gangs. But when he makes a big mistake and has an affair with White's mistress Bridget, he is set up and abandoned in a Mexican prison. His battle to work his way back to civilization will test all his skills. (2003)

Orhan Pamuk

My Name Is Red

In sixteenth-century Turkey, a gilder named Elegant is murdered. He had been employed by master miniaturist Enishte Effendi to work on a book celebrating the glories of the sultan. Then Enishte is also murdered. While the story of their deaths, and the possible explanations, are told from a fascinating blend of characters, the novel also displays the complex length and breath of this dying empire. Readers will be taken on a journey through religion, history, art, science, and love as the effect of a new style of painting created a challenge to the fundamentalism of this closed society. (2001)

T. Jefferson Parker

Silent Joe

Will Trona raised Joe after rescuing him from an orphanage despite the horrible acid scars that are a constant reminder of Joe's early life. Eventually, Joe Trona becomes an Orange County sheriff's deputy and also the bodyguard of his politically influential adopted father. When Will is murdered because of Joe's negligence, Joe seeks to hunt down Will's killer. The forces aligned against Joe's mission include a kidnapping, two murders, and the hidden past of his own adopted kin that may make Joe rethink his entire life. This novel was a Barry nominee and the winner of the Edgar Award for best novel. (2002)

Iain Pears

An Instance of the Fingerpost

It is 1663 in Oxford, and Dr. Robert Grove has been found poisoned. Although a young woman named Sarah Blundy has been accused, tried, and hung for the murder, to solve this murder, the reader must follow the stories of four separate characters. One is Anthony Wood, an Oxford historian, while another is Oxford mathematician Dr. John Wallis. From outside the cloistered walls of academia comes Marco da Cola, an Italian physician treating the Blundy family and Jack Prestcott, the son of a traitor and Sarah's lover. Each man will add a little flavor to the story before the reader can know the truth. (1998)

Arturo Perez-Reverte

The Club Dumas

Lucas Corso, book hunter, has the curse of bibliomania, and he would do anything to get his hands on the next great rare first edition. When famed collector Enrique Taillefer is found hung, a handwritten chapter forty-two from Alexandre Dumas' *The Three Musketeers* is found with his body. Corso is hired to validate the chapter. Corso finds he must travel across Europe to try to trace the origins of this document and to stay one step ahead of the villains who would change his adventure into a life-threatening quest to uncover a manuscript capable of conjuring Satan. (1996)

Jodi Picoult

Plain Truth

On a dairy farm in Lancaster, Pennsylvania, an Amish teenager named Katie Fisher supposedly gives birth to a baby that she is then accused of smothering. When Philadelphia lawyer Ellie Hathaway tries to develop a defense for the girl, she discovers that the girl denies not only the murder, but also the birth. Seeking to resolve her own personal feelings, Ellie moves in with the Fishers and then attempts to become the girl's guardian when her parents reject their own child. Eventually, when the case reaches the courtroom, the plain truth will be revealed. This novel was a Mary Higgins Clark Award nominee. (2000)

Richard Price

Samaritan

Ray Mitchell, a white former TV writer and coke addict, has returned to Dempsy, New Jersey, to reunite with his teenaged daughter and to volunteer as a writing instructor at a high school. When he is assaulted, his childhood friend, African American police detective Nerese Ammons, launches an investigation. What befuddles her is that Ray refuses to identify his assailants. As she probes into her friend's new life, she finds that choices he made since returning to his old hometown may have had good intentions but have had dramatic and negative consequences. (2003)

Elizabeth Redfern

The Music of Spheres

Jonathan Absey's daughter, a red-haired prostitute, has fallen victim to a serial killer. It is 1795, and the police are corrupt and ineffectual, while London itself is rife with international intrigue as the French Revolution continues to drive expatriates to the city. Perhaps one clue is Jonathan's work for the Home Office searching for spies in the government. Jonathan's half-brother, the gay amateur astronomer Alexander, decides to act as detective while he is also engaged in searching for a supposed secret in the sky. The question becomes how far will the timid half-brother go to protect and defend his family's virtue. (2001)

Alice Sebold

The Lovely Bones

Susie Salmon is the victim of a serial killer watching the consequences of her death from heaven. She sees her family cope with her death but eventually suffer the consequences of losing a loved one. Susie watches as her father tries to be brave and gather evidence needed to find her killer. She witnesses the descent of her mother into the abyss of coping with the death of her daughter. Her siblings try to go on with their lives living in the shadow of their missing sister. Even the boy who first kissed her has Susie as a watchful angel. After ten years of watching, Susie is able to have her wish granted and bring closure to this terrible incident in the lives of the Salmon family. This novel was a British Book Award and Bram Stoker Award winner. (2002)

Anita Shreve

The Weight of Water

Professional photographer Jean has traveled with her husband Thomas and daughter Billie to Smuttynose Island off the coast of New Hampshire on board a sailboat. Part of the reason for the trip is to save her marriage, but that becomes difficult when her brother-in-law Rick and his girlfriend Adaline's shipboard affair becomes strained. Jean obsesses on her assignment to investigate the axe murder of two women in 1873. When the eyewitness account of the crime becomes available to her, it provides a dangerous similar pathway for those struggling in modern times with the same loneliness. This novel was an Orange Prize for Fiction nominee and an L.L. Winship/PEN New England Award winner. (1997)

Martin Cruz Smith

Rose

American Jonathan Blair has spent his life on Africa's Gold Coast working as a mining engineer until 1872. When he is forced by circumstances to return to England for an extended amount of time, he becomes sullen and seeks solace in drink. His employer, Bishop Hannay, tries to engage him in an investigation into the disappearance of a curate named John Rowland from the coal-mining community of Wigan, Lancaster. Rowland was engaged to marry the bishop's daughter Charlotte, but no one in the small town seems willing to help Blair. Oddly, he finds himself partnered with the beautiful "pit girl" Rose Malyneaux, and their partnership may lead to the truth. This novel was a Hammett Award winner. (1996)

John Smolens

Cold

Norman Haas has been languishing in prison in Michigan's Upper Peninsula. When the opportunity arises, he escapes during a snowstorm to avenge himself on his own family, who sent him to prison. Through the harsh weather, he manages to make his way only by bringing tragedy to innocent people in his path, like Liesl Tiomenen, whom he abandons in a snowstorm. This sets Sheriff Del Maki on his trail. Reaching Noel Pronovost, the woman Norman still loves despite her betrayal, he is ready for the final confrontation. In a snow-covered setting, all the people he has hurt arrive to administer justice for his crimes. (2001)

Olen Steinhauer

The Bridge of Sighs

Emil Brod lives in a small, unnamed Eastern European country still occupied by Russian troops in 1948. As one of the youngest members of its police force, he is only twenty-two when he joins the homicide squad of the People's Militia. His first case involves the murder of a songwriter who writes patriotic songs about the occupied country. As Brod develops his case, he discovers that the songwriter might be Smerdyakov the Butcher, who committed atrocities under the Nazi occupation. This novel was an Edgar and Ellis Peters Historical Dagger nominee. (2003)

Donna Tartt

The Little Friend

It is twelve years since the murder of nine-year-old Robin Cleve Dufresnes, who was found dangling from a family tree in Alexandria, Mississippi. His family has disintegrated since his death, turning his mother into a recluse and driving his father from the family altogether. This has left his sisters, Harriet and Allison, to be raised by the family's African American maid, Ida Rhew, and their grandmother Edie. When little Harriet, just a baby at the time of her brother's death, decides to fix the family by focusing an investigation into her brother's murder on the hated low-life Danny Ratliff, she brings more danger to her home. This novel was an Orange Prize for Fiction nominee. (2002)

Donna Tartt
Secret History

Richard Papen has migrated from his blue-collar California home to the lush confines of Hampden College in Vermont. Joining a clique of students who spend their day quoting the Greeks, Richard is indoctrinated into their ritual of alcohol and pills. Then one night, his new friends reveal that they killed a man. Shortly thereafter, one student who wants to tell the truth is murdered as well. (1992)

David Thomson
Suspects

Written by a famous film critic, this novel begins as if it were an encyclopedia of movie characters, telling the reader what happened to them after their major film roles were over. But as the book progresses, characters from one film start showing up in the lives of characters from other films. Suddenly it becomes obvious that someone is narrating this story and changing film history as they do. (1985)

Darren Williams
Angel Rock

When Henry Gunn abandons his own sons at work in a moment of irresponsibility, thirteen-year-old Tom Ferry and his four-year-old half-brother Flynn go missing. Sheriff Pop Mather is unable to figure out what is going on and finds no comfort when a Sydney detective named Gibson arrives in the small Australian town of Angel Rock to try to seek the truth about another Angel Rock tragedy. Teenaged Darcy has slit her wrists and died in Sydney, and Gibson has been sent to find out why. Then unexpectedly, Tom returns to Angel Rock without his brother, silent and traumatized by his week in the desert. (2002)

Carlos Ruiz Zafon
The Shadow of the Wind

In Barcelona in the 1950s, Daniel Sempere is only eleven years old when he discovers the magic in a book called *The Shadow of the Wind* by Julián Carax. He cannot understand why a disfigured man called Laín Coubert, sharing the same name as the devil in Carax's book, is making it his obsession to destroy all the copies of the text. As he grows older, Daniel decides to investigate the life of Carax and Coubert, and this leads him into an alliance with some strange characters that may place his life in danger. (2001)

Appendix:
Sample Handout for a
Book Discussion

For each book discussion that you lead it is appropriate to create a handout for your group. The purpose of the handout is

- to provide the participants with information about the author for future reference,
- to provide a referral to other authors that the participants might enjoy, and
- to provide your contact information to the participants.

To be able to use an author photograph on your handout, I would suggest visiting the author's Web site. Most authors' Web sites provide a publicity photograph for use in promoting the author's work. If indicated, the photographer's name should be included on the handout. At the least, a credit should be given for the source of the photograph.

Biographical information about the author can also be obtained on the author's Web site. Quality biographical tools are available such as Gale's Literature Resource Center, which will provide needed author background. An Internet search on the author's name will reveal stored reviews, interviews, and news items that might be of interest to the readers.

Award information is available on most author's Web sites. See the introduction for a list of award sites.

To determine if a reader's guide exists on the Web for a particular title, do a search as follows:

- "author's name" "title of book" "reader's guide"

Substitute the words "book discussion questions" if "reader's guide" does not reveal a source.

For similar titles, do the same author and title search with the word "readalikes." Substitute the words "if you like" if "readalikes" does not reveal similar titles.

Photo courtesy of Lisa Balzo

Sandra Balzo

Uncommon Grounds

Sandra Balzo lives in Brookfield, Wisconsin, with her husband and two children. Sandra spent twenty years in public relations, publicity, and event management before forming her own public relations company, Balzo Communications. She is an active member of the fan mystery community and has worked on many of the Bouchercon: World Mystery Conventions. Her first short story, "The Grass Is Always Greener" (2003) was nominated for an Anthony Award and won the Robert L. Fish Award and a Macavity Award for Best Short Story. Her second story, "Viscery," was an Anthony nominee and won the Derringer Award.

Your Name and Your Contact Information

◇◇◆◇◇

Web site:
http://www.sandrabalzo.com

Reader's Guide:
http://www.sandrabalzo.com/
readinggroup.html

Readalikes

Donna Andrews

Cleo Coyle (Coffeehouse Mystery Series)

Dianne Mott Davidson

Joan Hess

Resources for Mystery and Crime Book Discussion Leaders

BOOKS

Balcom, Ted. *Book Discussions for Adults: A Leader's Guide.* ALA, 1992. 0–838–93413–7.

Charles, John with Joanna Morrison and Candace Clark. *The Mystery Readers' Advisory: The Librarian's Clues to Murder and Mayhem.* ALA, 2002. 0–838–90811–X.

Huang, Jim. *They Died in Vain: Overlooked, Underappreciated and Forgotten Mystery Novels.* Crum Creek Press, 2002. 0–962–58047–3.

Laskin, David. *The Reading Group Book: The Complete Guide to Starting and Sustaining a Reading Group, with Annotated Lists of 250 Titles for Provocative Discussion.* Plume, 1995. 0–452–27201–7.

McMains, Victoria Golden. *The Readers' Choice: 200 Book Club Favorites.* Quill, 2000. 0–688–17435–3.

Niebuhr, Gary Warren. *Make Mine a Mystery: A Reader's Guide to Mystery and Detective Fiction.* Libraries Unlimited, 2003. 1–563–08784–7.

Pearl, Nancy. *Book Lust: Recommended Reading for Every Mood, Moment and Reason.* Sasquatch Books, 2003. 1–570–61381–8.

Pearl, Nancy. *More Book Lust: Recommended Reading for Every Mood, Moment, and Reason.* Sasquatch Books, 2005. 1–570–61435–0.

Saal, Rollene. *The New York Public Library Guide to Reading Groups.* Crown, 1995. 0–517–88357–0.

INTERNET

Book Club How To's from the Seattle Public Library's Washington Center for the Book
http://www.spl.org/default.asp?pageID=collection_discussiongroup_howtos

Bookbrowse.com's Reading Guides for Book Clubs
    http://www.bookbrowse.com/reading_guides

The Bookmovement Essential Book Club Planner[TM]
    http://www.bookmovement.com/info/startabookclub.html

Random House's Book Group Corner
    http://www.randomhouse.com/resources/bookgroup/book_group_guide.html

ReadingGroupGuides.com: the Online Community for Reading Groups
    http://www.readinggroupguides.com

Author Index

Title Index

Subject Index

Location Index

Time Period Index

About the Author

GARY WARREN NIEBUHR is the Library Director for the Village of Greendale in Wisconsin. Gary operates P.I.E.S. (Private Investigator Entertainment Service), a mail-order catalog of private eye fiction at http://www.execpc.com/~piesbook/piescatalog.html. He is the author of *Make Mine a Mystery* (Libraries Unlimited, 2003), which won the Macavity Award, the Anthony Award, and The Kenneth Kingery Scholarly Book Award from the Council for Wisconsin Writers in 2004. He is also the author of *A Reader's Guide to the Private Eye Novel* (G. K. Hall, 1993), which was nominated for an Anthony Award. His private eye short story, "Over There," appears in the Summer 2004 issue of *Hardluck Stories*.

Gary received the Don Sandstrom Memorial Award for Lifetime Achievement in Mystery Fandom and he was the Fan Guest of Honor at the 2004 Bouchercon and at the 1995 Magna Cum Murder. He received the 2005 Margaret E. Monroe Award from the American Library Association in recognition of his contribution to the development of adult services in libraries.